Strategic Leadership of Change in Higher Education

D0221596

New initiatives to help organisations compete in the marketplace are being announced every day, be it a new IT system, new approaches to performance management or a new way of budgeting and forecasting. In today's higher education system, the multitude of external drivers have not only increased the pace of change but also forced senior management teams to reconceptualise the way various change initiatives should be managed.

Strategic Leadership of Change in Higher Education analyses the key features in planning, delivery and monitoring the impact of planned change initiatives in higher education. Drawing on the current research base on the management of change, it compares and contrasts the findings of 25 action research high level corporate change management projects. Initiatives discussed include:

- the introduction of Kaplan and Norton's 'Balanced Scorecard' approach, resulting in strategic mapping at all levels
- a major cultural shift programme to bring about globalisation of all aspects of the university, taking account of the different perspectives as to how this should be achieved
- the introduction of a mentoring scheme to promote diversity and equality, and to promote greater understanding and support of black and ethnic minority staff.

Packed with practical lessons for leadership and change in higher education, this book raises awareness as to how to tackle topical issues and effectively lead universities through major change. With expert commentary and feedback from the stakeholders involved at each institution, *Strategic Leadership of Change in Higher Education* is essential reading for all those taking on leadership and management positions in higher education.

Stephanie Marshall is Director of Programme Development at the Leadership Foundation for Higher Education and was previously a Provost at the University of York, working in the Centre for Leadership and Management.

Strategic Leadership of Change in Higher Education

What's new?

Edited by Stephanie Marshall

 Routledge
Taylor & Francis Group

LONDON AND NEW YORK

First published 2007
by Routledge
2 Park Square, Milton Park, Abingdon, Oxon OX14 4RN

Simultaneously published in the USA and Canada
by Routledge
270 Madison Ave, New York, NY 10016

Routledge is an imprint of the Taylor & Francis Group, an informa business

Typeset in Times New Roman by
RefineCatch Limited, Bungay, Suffolk
Printed and bound in Great Britain by
The Cromwell Press, Trowbridge, Wiltshire

British Library Cataloguing in Publication Data
A catalogue record for this book is available from the British Library

Library of Congress Cataloging-in-Publication Data
A catalog record for this book has been requested

ISBN10: 0–415–41172–6 (hbk)
ISBN10: 0–415–41173–4 (pbk)
ISBN10: 0–203–96285–0 (ebk)

ISBN13: 978–0–415–41172–1 (hbk)
ISBN13: 978–0–415–41173–4 (pbk)
ISBN13: 978–0–203–96285–0 (ebk)

Contents

Figures

Tables

Contributors

Yahya Al-Nakeeb started his lecturing career following completion of his PhD in sports science at Birmingham University in 1979. He has over 25 years of working experience at various institutions of Higher Education in this country and abroad. Currently, he is the Director of Research and Head of Sports Studies at Newman College of Higher Education. His research interests span across both theoretical and applied domains of physical education, sports science, psychology and education with particular interest in psycho-physiological aspects of physical activity and children's health and fitness. He is a strong advocate of collaborative endeavour in research and scholarship.

Uduak Archibong is the Director for the Centre for Inclusion and Diversity, at the University of Bradford. She leads the development of Diversity and Inclusion in Learning, Teaching and Assessment in the University of Bradford. Her research, teaching and knowledge transfer activities broadly cover the areas of workforce diversity, leadership development, family-centred health care and cross-cultural negotiation of community/family access to, and engagement in health and social services.

Barbara Burford is Deputy Director for the Centre for Inclusion and Diversity at the University of Bradford. She is also CEO of Barbara Burford Consulting Limited. A former NHS Research Scientist and Senior Civil Servant, she has been Director of Diversity for the Department for Work and Pensions and Head of Equalities for the NHS at the Department of Health.

Julian Constable is currently a lecturer in Education at Suffolk College in Ipswich. He graduated in Sociology and has worked on research projects investigating industry and higher education links. He has developed an interest in the changing nature of the post-compulsory sector of education in relation to management structures in recent years in both the FE and HE areas. He also has an interest in pedagogical issues in further and higher education.

Simon Donoghue is Head of the Project Management Group, University of Leeds. He has overall responsibility for leading a team of Project Managers and Officers, providing high level project management, change management and interim leadership capability to drive forward strategic priorities. Simon also guides a multi-functional project team responsible for facilitating the development and implementation of the University's strategy, using strategy map and balanced score card principles. Prior to working at the University of Leeds, Simon was a strategic project manager for the Leeds and Holbeck Building Society and Senior Lecturer in Operations Management, at the University of Huddersfield.

Kevin Edge, FREng, has been Pro-Vice-Chancellor for Research at the University of Bath since 2003 and Deputy Director of the Centre for Power Transmission and Motion Control since 1992. As Pro-Vice-Chancellor, Kevin has responsibility for the development and implementation of the University's research strategy, the formation of research policy and procedures, and all matters relating to the Research Assessment Exercise. Externally, he serves on the HERDA-SW Executive Committee and Research Special Interest Group. He is also a Director of Emerson's Innovations Ltd and member of the SetSquared Partnership Board. He is a Fellow of the LFHE TMP Programme.

Paul Evans is Director of Business Excellence at Liverpool John Moores University. He has more than 20 years' experience of management innovation in both industry and higher education. He has worked extensively with the European Foundation for Quality Management (EFQM). A senior assessor for the European Quality Award since 2001, he has also spoken frequently on the subject of management excellence at UK and European conferences. He is a fellow of the Chartered Institute of Personnel and Development and an Associate of the Institute of Quality Assurance.

Patricia Gayá Wicks joined the University of Exeter as a lecturer in Leadership Studies in 2006. Her recently completed doctoral work focused on how leaders can take effective action in the face of overwhelming circumstances, most particularly as in the case of our current ecological crisis. As a member of the Centre for Leadership Studies, Patricia teaches on the undergraduate Management with Leadership programme, the MA/MRes in Leadership Studies programmes, and on CPD courses. Patricia was awarded her PhD at the University of Bath, where she also held the position of Project Officer supporting the LFHE Fellowship awarded to Professor Edge.

Paul Gentle is Dean of International Education and Director of Regional Affairs at The College of St Mark and St John, Plymouth. Paul has responsibility for developing the international and regional profile of the college. He manages a School of 15 staff, running programmes in teacher and trainer development, leadership and management. Paul is also Director of Regional

Affairs, and works to develop the College's relations with local business and community organisations. His current research interests include the management of change, and strategic leadership in higher education.

Lynne Howlett is Newcastle University's Leadership and Management Development Adviser. Current projects include exploring succession management for senior leaders at Newcastle and a Collaborative Academic Leaders Programme with Durham University and the Leadership Foundation. Lynne is also contributing to a number of sector working groups looking at succession management for leaders in Higher Education. Lynne holds a degree in English from Newcastle University, a Postgraduate Certificate in Human Resource Management and is a Fellow of the Chartered Institute of Personnel and Development.

Stephanie Marshall is Director of Programme Development at the Leadership Foundation for Higher Education (LFHE), where she has had responsibility for the National Mentoring Scheme, developing and delivering the suite of executive programmes (e.g. Senior Strategic Leadership, Preparing for Senior Strategic Leadership and Heads of Departments), the 31 HEIs in the north of England and the Leadership Foundation Fellowship Programme (LFFP) since June 2004. Round One of the latter initiative, the LFFP (one of the LFHE's Flagship Projects), has already made a significant impact, with some of the projects (written up for the purposes of this volume) recognised globally as offering interesting and useful models of change.

Prior to her present post, Stephanie was a Provost at the University of York and worked in the Centre for Leadership and Management in the Department of Management Studies. She has an active interest in educational and leadership and management development research, continuing to teach, research and publish. She is the co-editor, with Heather Fry and Steve Ketteridge, of two high-sales Routledge text books: *Teaching and Learning in HE: Enhancing Academic Practice* (currently being updated into 3rd edition) and *The Effective Academic* (2002) and has published numerous articles and chapters in books on pedagogy, leadership and management of change.

Bob Munn is Vice-President for Teaching and Learning at the University of Manchester, where he is responsible for policy in the area of teaching, learning and assessment, and for academic quality and standards. He was previously Professor of Chemical Physics at UMIST, where he also served five years as Dean. He chairs the Steering Group on Benchmarking of the Quality Assurance Agency for Higher Education and acts as an institutional auditor for QAA. He is a member of the National Advisory Panel for the National Teaching Fellowship Project Scheme run by the Higher Education Academy.

Teresa Rees is a member of the Department for Trade and Industry's Steering

Group advising on the setting up of the Commission for Equality and Human Rights. She has also served as an Equal Opportunities Commissioner for Wales. She received a CBE for service to equality and higher education.

Malcolm Rhodes is Pro-Vice-Chancellor (Academic) and a member of the senior management team at the University of Chester. He has responsibility for learning and teaching, quality and standards and a range of academic services, including learning resources, Academic Registry and information technology services. Formerly employed at a senior level in production management in industry, Dr Rhodes holds postgraduate qualifications in education management and a doctorate from the University of Durham.

Chris Shiel is currently Head of Learning at the Institute of Business and Law, Bournemouth University (BU). She has led and contributed to a variety of strategic initiatives at Bournemouth, including championing the development of 'global perspectives' and leading strategic approaches to e-learning. At a national level, she has contributed to change through the Development Education Association (as Chair of the HE Committee and Council Member) and through the Association of Business Schools. Through Chris's work, the University is recognised as a leader in the development of a holistic approach to sustainability.

Tony Stevenson is Newcastle University's Pro-Vice-Chancellor for Planning and Resources. He is responsible for the University's financial/resource planning. Tony's Leadership Foundation Fellowship allowed the university to pilot Development Centres for succession management at Newcstle. He has subsequently become even more engaged with leadership development as a steering group member for the University's Academic Leaders Programme. Tony has a BSc in Botany/Zoology and a PhD in Botany. His research interests are in recent environmental change in the European uplands, history of interaction between humans, climate and vegetation in the western Mediterranean, and the history of woodland management in the Mediterranean region.

Helen Valentine is currently Pro-Vice-Chancellor at Anglia Ruskin University. She has responsibility for HR and Student Experience issues. Prior to this she worked at UWE in Bristol where she was Associate Dean and then Dean of Bristol Business School before taking on the role of Assistant Vice-Chancellor. Helen studied Food Science then spent ten years as a manager in industry before gaining her MBA from Warwick University. She has developed an interest in Leadership, Governance and Management issues and has served on the HEFCE LGM committee and acts as an assessor for the HEFCE LGM Fund.

Gwen Wileman has been employed at DMU as Director of HR since 2001. She has significant experience as HR Director in a range of organisations including a large progressive university, the NHS and a range of Post Office businesses. She has experience as a senior manager in a progressive training and development organisation and academic experience as a Senior Lecturer in HRM in a Business School designated as a Centre of Excellence. She is Midlands Regional Chair of the University Personnel Association and a member of the National Executive Committee.

Hannah Young is Equality and Diversity Manager at Cardiff University. She previously worked as a Diversity Officer at the University of Oxford.

Preface

At the heart of this book is a series of compelling stories of change, told with honesty and enthusiasm, and all containing immensely practical lessons for leadership and change in higher education. Taken as a whole, they are also a chapter in the story of the initial phase of the Leadership Foundation for Higher Education (LFHE), which was created in early 2004 to define and meet the development needs of leaders, managers and governors across the UK's 160 universities and higher education colleges.

I had come into this role in 2004 from running the Civil Service College at Sunningdale, now the National School of Government. When I was at Sunningdale, I commissioned a major piece of research through the Chartered Institute of Personnel and Development and undertaken by Professor Sue Richards at the School of Public Policy at the University of Birmingham, into what were the key factors that determined successful leadership in the public sector. This piece of qualitative research sought out leaders who were perceived as successful from a wide range of areas including education, local government, central government, health, the police and other front-line delivery services. It then uncovered through their telling of their stories what they thought these key characteristics were, and further evidence came from additional sets of interviews with those who worked with them and other stakeholders.

One characteristic that so many of them had in common was the capacity to tell stories very effectively about their own area of responsibility or organisation. These stories took two forms. In most cases, since the organisations were going through a major process of change, they were very effective at telling the story of change, the sense of direction and mode of travel, and the challenges that the change process would bring with it. Equally, as change processes rolled out, they were also extremely effective at telling the stories of success from within their own part of the organisation, or indeed from other parts of it. In short, the processes of narrative, conversation and dialogue were absolutely essential to their sense of purpose and achievement as leaders, and to their credibility as deliverers of change.

This has reinforced a growing working assumption of my own that the process of leadership development must be closely interwoven with storytelling within organisations. The art of telling stories effectively is, after all, one that pivots around engaging the attention of others. And that term, 'engaging', is a very critical one. When the Leadership Foundation for Higher Education first developed its Strategic Plan in 2004, we decided to produce a working 'strap line'. We opted not to use phrases such as 'equipping tomorrow's leaders' or 'building capacity in higher education'. Instead, we simply used the phrase 'engaging with leaders in higher education'. This process of engagement, underpinned by storytelling and narrative, seems hugely important in creating a culture and climate for change, whether in an organisation or a whole sector, and it helps give doubters the confidence to see the change process through.

I hope this approach will also start to change some of the unhelpful rhetoric of change management that in recent years has developed fairly 'macho' phrases such as 'driving reform' and 'confronting the blockers' and encouraged super structures of bewildering quantitative targets. None of this is aiming to make the process of change management softer, as there has to be clarity of purpose and indeed an appropriate number of clear and believable targets. The issue is the narrative that is wrapped around the process of change. It needs to be a believable narrative and one that is absolutely right for the organisation in question. There is no 'one size fits all' in this business of change management. And the stories in this book demonstrate the power of that process.

Creating and developing the Leadership Foundation for Higher Education has itself been a change management process. When we were set up, many believed we could not make a difference. We had to develop our own compelling narrative, and define a journey and a process that others would buy into and believe in. It was very rewarding that, in the review undertaken by our four Funding Councils at the end of our first two-and-a-half years (in Spring 2006), we received a very powerful endorsement for the programme of work we were undertaking and how we were doing it. In particular, the assessment congratulated us on the way in which we were engaging with institutions and leaders within and across higher education.

It was a unique process in early 2004 to be presented with almost a blank sheet, combined with useful start-up funding and a requirement to develop a business that would eventually become sustainable. We therefore had the opportunity, in addition to developing programmes that people would pay to attend, to invest in the sector to encourage a greater focus on organisational and leadership development.

It is interesting to reflect now on how we chose to invest a very substantial part of our funding in the Fellowships Scheme. In the original thinking, the idea had been that we would perhaps have a leadership and management Awards Scheme, where we would invite applications and commendations about good practice in leadership, management and governor development and sit in judgement over them and reward the best with the equivalent of the 'Oscars'. However, we somehow felt that this would not make the active contribution to the development of practice and innovation that we intended. At this point, we were extremely grateful to one of our Board members, Professor Katharine Perera, then Pro-Vice-Chancellor of the University of Manchester, who conceived almost in one single dialogue with us the idea of the Fellowships. What emerged was that we wanted a process that enabled us to be much more proactive in working with those who are striving for excellence in organisational and leadership development. We wanted very high standards from the outset and that led to a very rigorous process of selection of the many applications that far outnumbered the available places. We also put in place the arrangements to coach each of the Fellows and their project teams. We ensured that there was a very good interaction between them and other Fellows and indeed others who were leading development processes within the Leadership Foundation.

As we put our strategy together, the idea of the Fellowships fitted very well. On the one hand, a lot of our developing programmes were focused on individual leaders coming together outside their institutions, linking with colleagues from other HEIs or indeed other sectors. The flagship programme of that kind was, and still is, our Top Management Programme, now supplemented by many other such open programmes for various levels and specialities of leadership within higher education. On the other hand, it was critical to enter the process through the lens of the organisation and through teams, whether senior management groups or project teams. The Fellowships have enabled us to do that. They have also brought together this enormously rich array of material which is now set out in this book. It also underlined a very important principle to which I hold dearly, namely that the best material for leadership development is not carefully constructed, 'disembodied case studies' but the real issues of running the organisation. The Fellowship projects are rooted in 'bread and butter' issues of teaching and learning, research, restructuring, diversity, internationalisation and enhancing the student experience. The smaller the gap is between doing the job of leadership and learning about it, the more effective it is perceived to be and the more likely individuals are to find the time to do it.

The opening chapter by Professor Stephanie Marshall brings together many of the main themes from these stories. I would just like to reflect on a few others that seem very important to me, in addition to the concept of the story or narrative that I have already mentioned.

The first theme that comes through so strongly from many of the stories is continuously to recognise the importance of distributed leadership at all levels of the organisation. Inherent in that is not just recognising its existence, but also acknowledging when it has to be counter-balanced by a strong corporate leadership from the top, particularly in the role of championing change. One of the projects also advocates very strongly the diagonal slice in the project team, which cuts across levels. This is something we particularly encourage in the change project teams in the Change Academy, which we run jointly with the Higher Education Academy.

Second, what comes across very strongly is about 'striking the right balance'. This is particularly the case in the project that used the 'right touch' approach, balancing rigour with clarity, with bureaucracy and with speed. Indeed, it is very encouraging that one of the projects used the balanced scorecard approach.

Third, all the change management literature emphasises the huge importance of persistent and focused communication. What so many of these projects bring out, is that that is not just a one-way process, but a persistent engagement with stakeholders, both internally and externally, from one end of the change process to the other.

Fourth, it is good to identify in many of the projects how important it is to establish internal networks that underpin the change process. We at the Leadership Foundation have found the power of networks as learning organisations. Often the most effective way to create these within an organisation is of course through action learning techniques.

Finally, it is good to see so many practical and pragmatic messages coming through these stories. Maintaining a sense of momentum and focus on a major project is often a highly stressful activity involving quite a lot of disappointment and set backs. Perhaps the most important ingredient to weather that particular storm is maintaining your sense of humour and, ideally, sharing it with others.

Overall, our Fellows have added enormous value to the Leadership Foundation, and we are extremely grateful to all of them. They have enriched our own thinking, made strong links across to other areas of our work, such as the research and small development projects, and are helping us to underpin our main work with powerful evidence of practice.

We now have a second cohort of Fellows who are working on an equally rigorous and leading-edge set of projects. Together, these two cohorts represent a powerful set of alumni of the Leadership Foundation and I am sure we will find opportunities to encourage continuing sharing of information and outcomes.

We owe our thanks to a number of key individuals. First and foremost, as I have already mentioned, the idea of the Fellowships was very much the inspiration of Professor Katharine Perera, a member of the Leadership Foundation Board. She has not only enriched the thinking as we had developed the concept, but played an active part in setting the rigorous standards that underpin the scheme and chairing the selection team for both cohorts. Equal and enthusiastic thanks are also due to Professor Stephanie Marshall, Editor of this important book, and Project Director throughout the Leadership Foundation Fellowships Programme. She has brought, above all, a tremendous sense of enthusiasm and excitement which has encouraged

Fellows to deliver to the high standards of quality which they have. She has also ensured that they were properly supported by our Associates acting in a coaching role. She has made sure that links are made between the outcomes of these Fellowships and our other work, whether the main open programmes which she runs or other parts of our activity of a research and developmental nature. Thanks are also due for the huge commitment given by Sarah Hubbard, Project Officer at the Leadership Foundation, who has supported this project from the outset.

The first cohort of Fellows was launched very engagingly by Lord Patten, Chancellor of the Universities of Oxford and Newcastle. At the very successful Dissemination Event that followed about nine months later, we are hugely indebted to Dame Rennie Fritchie (then Commissioner for Public Appointments) for her inspiring address to the group. These contributions were equally important in giving the right profile to the whole programme and ensuring a high level of commitment. As more than one of the project reports say, the fact that it was linked to a national scheme run by the Leadership Foundation was a factor in the success of making it happen within their institution.

Across its wide range of programmes, I can give the commitment that the Leadership Foundation will continue to strive to make sure that the stories of change continue to be told, that narratives develop and that vital transformational change across HE is effectively implemented as a consequence.

Ewart Wooldridge CBE

Acknowledgements

The editor wishes to acknowledge all those who have assisted in the production of this book. A big thanks to the twelve contributing authors, who all undertook to write up their projects into chapter form whilst juggling a myriad of other projects. I am especially grateful to my boss, Ewart Wooldridge CBE, and Sarah Hubbard, Project Officer, both of the Leadership Foundation for Higher Education, who provided much encouragement and ongoing support.

Finally, I must thank Luci and Joe for allowing me so much undisturbed time in my study, and, as always, for being so supportive and understanding.

Chapter 1

Leading and managing strategic change

Stephanie Marshall

> It is not the strongest of the species that survives, nor the most intelligent;
> it is the one that is most adaptable to change.
>
> Charles Darwin

Context

Not a day goes by without some new initiative being announced that some-one, somewhere, thinks will make a major difference to an organisation's ability to be even more competitive in the market place. Be it new IT systems, new approaches to performance management, new value adding processes, or new ways of budgeting and forecasting, someone somewhere will perceive one or more of these as providing a potentially more efficient and effective means of realising corporate objectives. In today's higher education system, the multitude of external drivers (e.g. globalisation, the introduction of student fees, e-learning) have not only increased the pace of change, but also forced senior management teams to reconceptualise the way in which various change initiatives should be led and managed.

The beginning of the twenty-first century heralded a marked shift in the analysis of what constitutes effective leadership. No longer is 'heroic' leadership deemed to be the 'panacea' that an organisation's board or appointing body seeks (Collins 2001, Boyatzis and McKee 2005). Instead, the idea of dispersed leadership, or 'leadership at all levels' is seen as a more appropriate means of bringing about and sustaining transformational and lasting change. This is achieved through a cadre of committed and passionate leaders 'owning' the goals of both continuous improvement and on-going learning. These 'new leaders' recognise that change is not just an event, i.e. something that after its announcement becomes a reality, but rather a transition, often lengthy, which requires careful planning and execution (Bridges 2005). Additionally – and this is the aspect that many under-performing 'leaders' balk at – to take on such a leadership role requires visibility and presence. Time needs to be created for constant monitoring of the transition process – not just of quantitative indicators, but of the mood of the personnel key to the delivery of the proposed changed mode of operating and/or behaving.

By and large it is now accepted that organisations cannot afford to 'stand still'. The 'no change' option is actually not an option. With increased competitiveness (to include organisations looking to find their own 'niche' market) combined with greater capabilities in strategic planning (to include a better sense of determining mission critical strategies for a range of operational areas) more senior staff are engaging with the thorny issue of how best to bring about transformational, embedded and lasting change that will ensure their organisation not only survives, but thrives.

Despite a recognised body of research generated from the private sector as to what makes for effective change management (Kanter *et al.* 1992, Kotter 1996, Bridges 2005), higher education institutions (HEIs) continue to suggest that their needs are different to those of the private sector, as their culture is so different (Weil 1994, Slowey 1995). However, as HEIs seek to redefine the balance of income generated from public and private sources (Shattock 2003), HE can no longer be considered in solely public sector terms nor thus very different to the commercial sector. Rather, it should be seen as a 'hybrid' (private, public and not for profit). The push, now, is for institutions serious about competing in the marketplace to become more commercially minded in terms of 'running the business'.

The 'art', then, of leading and managing change in HE is high on the institutional and individual developmental agenda further to this need to achieve competitive advantage. Part of this 'art' is to consider the appropriate infrastructure (i.e. value adding processes, rigorous underpinning systems, and performance management metrics) for the change process. There are lessons to be learned here from the private sector, both good and bad. However, as the research findings which follow show, 'it ain't so different in HE' as some like to suggest.

What follows is an analysis of key features in planning, delivery and monitoring the impact of planned change initiatives in HE. Incorporated are comparisons and contrasts with the existing literature generated from the private sector. The analysis results from the evaluation reports written up by key senior staff in 25 UK HEIs. These key senior individuals, 'Leadership Foundation Fellowship Programme Fellows' (LFFP Fellows) were selected via a competitive process and awarded up to £40,000 by the LFHE in 2005 in support of delivery of their proposed nine month project (see Box 1.1).

The evaluation reports written up at the end of the nine month period for which funding was granted informs the analysis which follows.

Background

Prior to considering the key features of effective change management in HE, it is worth visiting the frameworks provided by two 'gurus' of change

Box 1.1 Leadership Foundation Fellowships Programme awards to institutions

Anglia Ruskin University
Change at the top: an evaluation of major changes to leadership, management and university structures

College of St Mark and St John
Towards a learning organisation: capacity building in business and community engagement

DeMontfort University
HR transformation – a new service model

Kingston University
Developing integrated student support

Liverpool John Moores
Management by processes and facts

London Business School
Embedding diversity in leadership and management at the LBS

London South Bank University
Wider management mentoring programme for women and ethnic minority managers

Napier University
Administrative professional practice in a learning environment

Newman College of Higher Education
Leading change in scholarship and research

Queen Mary, University of London
The leadership, management and governance of international collaborative academic projects

University of Bath
Encouraging, supporting and embedding collaborative research across HEIs

University of Bournemouth
Developing and embedding of 'global perspectives' across the university curriculum

University of Bradford
Cultural understanding in leadership and management

University of Cardiff
Project to enhance equality and diversity procedures within the university

University College, Chester
From management to leadership

University of Edinburgh
Academic leadership and strategic management project

University of Leeds
Leadership and strategy

University of Manchester
Conversational, not confrontational: a new approach to quality

University of Newcastle
Developing potential leaders

University of Oxford
Improving leadership, management and administration

University of Portsmouth
Achieving change by the back door

University of Reading
I-opener: a project to connect the service and academic departmental sides of IT and IS

University of Wales, Aberystwyth
Managing institutional review and change in connection with an application for degree awarding powers

University of Wales, Lampeter
TRUSST: the road to a university service strategy

University of Warwick
A process of developmental engagement between the university and students' union

management in the private sector – Rossabeth Moss Kanter and John Kotter (see Boxes 1.2 and 1.3). Certainly, both of these frameworks appear to apply not only to the private sector, from where they were derived, but also the HE sector. Both emphasise the importance of a vision and its communication, moving on to the notion of galvanising action which requires harnessing and consolidation and, ultimately, reinforcement. Kanter *et al.* hint at a more structured approach to the planning and roll-out of the change initiative (despite her normally being categorised as emphasising a 'softer', more people-focused approach to management – not that the two are

Box 1.2   Kanter *et al.* (1992) 'Commandments for bringing about lasting change'

1   Analyse the organisation and its need for change
2   Create a shared vision and common direction
3   Separate this vision from the past
4   Create a sense of urgency
5   Support a strong leadership role
6   Line up political sponsorship
7   Devise and monitor an implementation plan
8   Develop enabling structures
9   Communicate, involve people and be honest
10   Reinforce and institutionalise change.

Box 1.3   Kotter's (1996) 'eight-stage process'

1   Establish a sense of urgency
2   Create a guiding coalition
3   Develop a vision and strategy
4   Communicate the change vision
5   Empower employees for broad-based action
6   Generate short-term wins
7   Consolidate gains and produce more change
8   Anchor new approaches in the culture.

incompatible). Kotter, on the other hand, hints at the prospect of dispersed leadership, with individuals empowered to deliver the change. Combining the two provides a framework approximating to that arising from the HE study – i.e. a planned approach combined with an emphasis on leadership and attention to people, communication and support. So, let's unpack the HE data further.

Change in the UK higher education sector

What is interesting about the pointers for planning and delivering change in higher education (derived from the 25 evaluation reports) (see Box 1.4) is that it is so similar to those derived by Kanter and Kotter in the private sector over a decade ago. The one notable addition to the 'educators' list is point 12 – 'learn from experience'. This was a specific area that all the Fellows were asked to consider in their project evaluations. Many noted that this is the area

Box 1.4 LFFP Fellows' 13 pointers for planning and delivering change

Planning stage

1   Identify what needs to change.
2   Determine leadership and the ability to state the 'goal' clearly.
3   Deliver a clear vision.
4   Identify significant steps in the change process.
5   Avoid undue haste.
6   Determine how to align people behind the change – identify change agents and resistors.
7   Inspire confidence by:
     forestalling problems (planning for contingencies); and determining the means of monitoring and regular communication.

Actioning the change strategy

8   Provide leadership and build the team – develop trust, show compassion and understanding to casualties. Be as open and honest as you can.
9   Communicate throughout – explain, listen, ensure understanding, question, guide, acknowledge feelings and seek feedback.
10 Involve people- seek and develop commitment, participation, motivation and ownership.
11 Seek and celebrate early successes.

Monitoring and evaluation

12 Learn from experience.
13 Plan continuous improvement.

that normally gets overlooked with change projects, as time for reflection appears to become a 'luxury' in the rapid pace of day-to-day life in HE. The 'learning points' from the Fellows projects are explored in a later section, further to consideration of three distinct differences in the 'approach to inform the change' strategy.

Managing change in HE: what works well?

Overall, there were three distinct approaches to leading and managing the 25 change projects which underpinned the change strategy:

- devising a *structured framework* for managing change;
- *incentivising* the change process;
- *capacity building* to bring about change.

Each of these are considered in turn below.

Structured framework for managing change

A number of the projects used a top-down, strategically planned approach to managing change. Broad parameters were determined by the senior management team, with the phases of the change process predetermined. Subsequently staff were brought in (by a range of means: e.g. consultative e-mail process, focus groups, hierarchical dissemination) to engage and determine the 'filling-in of the detail'. This follows Bullock and Batten's (1985) planned approach to change which draws on the discipline of project management. They suggest a four-staged approach:

1   the *analysis stage*, considering 'where are we now' to explore the distance (i.e. 'gap' analysis) required to get to the desired changed state;
2   the *planning stage*, which they suggest should include contingency plans;
3   the *action stage* further to the agreed plan, within a monitoring and feedback framework;
4   the *integration stage*, which should result from the change strategy having been successfully completed.

Interestingly, this is an approach which to a certain extent could be seen to have been encouraged by the LFHE in that the guidelines which the Fellows were expected to follow included the submission of a detailed project management template. However, it is interesting to note that only just over half chose to use the structured framework approach to managing change.

Bullock and Batten's second phase – i.e. the planning stage – is a tricky one (not that the others aren't). In many organisations, a senior member of staff articulates a vision for the future and subsequently, aided by the senior management team and perhaps a few significant others, a strategy is drawn up based on a 'gap' analysis (not always as rigorously carried out as it could be). This approach often fails to take sufficient account of what Johnson and Scholes (2005) call the 'cultural web'. Building on this cultural web to better assess hard and soft indicators of the culture (see Figure 1.1) provides useful multi-dimensional data with respect to the cultural anatomy. This can help gauge whether or not the proposed vision, strategy and time scale are actually realistic.

The structured framework approach tended to be used where the change initiatives were focused primarily on administrative staff. For the LFFP Fellows wishing to engage academic staff and convince them of the merits of

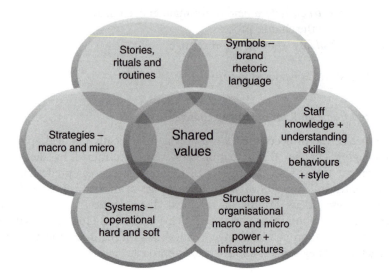

Figure 1.1 Cultural anatomy.

Source: Adapted from Johnson and Scholes 2005

the proposed change (often likened to herding cats), the incentivised or capacity building approaches were deemed more suitable.

The positive aspects of the structured framework approach focus on clarity. Clarity results from a concern to determine an appropriate timeframe, milestones, what requires to be done, who should be doing what when – in essence, the 'route map'. This clearly appeals to those with a preference for structures, logic and left brain activity. The negative aspects of this approach are congruent with Mintzberg's (1994) critique of the structured approach to strategic planning, i.e. it can only work in a stable, unchanging environment, and is insufficiently flexible to take account of emergent challenges. However, the research evidence from this study would suggest that with significant regard being paid to risk analysis and contingency planning, the risk of 'inflexiblity' was identified alongside the means of addressing it in plans for implementation.

Incentivised approach to change

An incentivised approach is one where 'carrots' are offered to encourage staff to take part in a proposed 'change' initiative. It was observed that in those projects which used this approach, commitment to the goal appeared to move beyond initial mere compliance to the gaining of a number of key champions to assist with subsequent promotion of the change. This approach was used where the change initiative didn't so much represent a change from what was, but rather represented the need to create something that wasn't. Such a tactic would appear to align with the philosophy of Nadler and Tushman's (1997) congruence model, which incorporates an understanding of the dynamics of an organisation during the change management process. This model suggests there are four co-dependant components of an organisation:

- the *formal organisation*
- the *informal organisation*
- the *work*
- the *people*.

They suggest that effective management of change requires addressing all four aspects and keeping them in balance. Therefore, if the change represents a new mode of operating, or 'work', that people do not recognise as part of either the formal or informal culture of the organisation, a means of getting some movement to shift the culture has to be found.

What staff believe the strategy to be is less critical than the unconscious strategies which become played out in organisational behaviours. Thus (and this is the approach that some of the Fellows found to be a way of bringing about the change in a short period of time), 'incentivisation' became the means of changing the 'work' of a proportion of the people by generating new organisational behaviours. This subsequently created 'pockets' of change, impacting on and creating a mixed economy within the informal organisation. This, in turn (it was envisaged), would be capable of bringing about systemic change in the formal organisation.

Finding the right incentives to engage staff in projects, or to undertake work which is outwith their terms of contract can initially prove difficult, particularly in a cash-strapped semi-publicly funded organisation. However by focusing on what motivates staff – incentives should be able to be found. Most commonly used incentives are illustrated in Table 1.1.

The plus side of such an approach is that to promote the change, the focus is on working with those who are positive about what is being proposed. Thus

Table 1.1 Motivating incentives

Time	E.g. sabbaticals or study leave, 'buy out' of certain activities, flexi-time
Training and development	E.g. in-house or external programmes, conferences, mentoring and/or coaching
Recognition	E.g. highlighting individual's an expertise, seeing one's name in print associated with a successful project
Status	E.g. providing the title of 'project manager', 'looks good on the cv' (more usual nowadays with an increasing number of institutions taking 'citizenship' seriously in terms of criteria for promotion)
Pump priming	E.g. especially in the case of projects gaining external funding

positive energy is created around the change initiative. However, the down side of such an approach is obvious – i.e. where there are 'winners', there are usually 'losers'. With a fixed pot of incentives, not everyone will be a beneficiary. Tied to this is that where there is non-engagement, there can also be cynicism. However, like all risks, if such factors are thought through rigorously in the planning stage, and if there is a sufficient potential critical mass to proceed with this approach, there can be some 'quick wins' to generate positive publicity for the change intitiative.

Capacity building

This approach is typified by the successful joint Leadership Foundation for Higher Education (LFHE) and Higher Education Academy (HEA) 'Change Academy' programme. This methodology involves a five-stage process: first, start with a clear goal; second, work with a team of the committed few; third, roll out a 'pilot'; fourth, disseminate the outcomes and the learning; and, finally, push to gain more recruits via the 'snowball' effect.

Edgar Schein (1992), building on the work of Kurt Lewin, sees change as being a three-stage process:

1   unfreezing, by creating a motivation to change;
2   learning new concepts and new meaning from old concepts;
3   internalising new concepts and meanings.

The capacity building approach is not so dissimilar in that using such a process with willing 'recruits' (i.e. those motivated to change), this change process is capable of producing 'change agents' (i.e. those capable of influencing and bringing others into the change process), thus bringing about a critical mass to take forward the change initiative and unfreeze others. Duck (1993) proposed the notion of using 'Transition Management Teams', or TMTs, to commit all their time and energy to managing change, disbanding only when the process has been embedded. This technique, she suggests, addresses the issue of 'change survivors': people who have devised clever strategies for surviving change programmes without actually changing. The capacity building approach – with its emphasis on teamwork – offers a useful means of 'squeezing out' these 'change survivors'. Eventually they are forced to become fully engaged or to fully opt out.

Further positive aspects of this approach are that the process becomes equally as important as the outputs for some of the team. Great commitment, enthusiasm and loyalty not only to the goals but also to the team which drives the collective forward. However, the down side is that some people can become too focused on the process and not sufficiently focused on the outputs, thus holding up progress towards goals. Once again, undertaking rigorous risk analysis during the planning stage should help determine if this

Table 1.2 Three approaches to managing change in HE

	Advantages	Disadvantages
A structured framework	• Clear route map – where planning is essential • Easy to determine milestones • Can 'pace' the change • Fixed target date for 'going live' easier to determine	• Can be overly ambitious/time frame too tight • Insufficient participant ownership • Can demotivate staff who are unable to keep up with the pace
An incentivised approach	• Can get engagement where it might otherwise have been impossible • Motivating for participants • Good to gain early wins	• Subsequent participants may not want to engage without the incentive: i.e. sets a precedent • High on resource implications • Pace of change may be slow
Capacity building	• Promotes teamwork and teambuilding • High motivation and commitment to succeed • Energising for those engaged with the process	• Pace of change may be slow • Resource implications of facilitating support for this approach • May result in too great an emphasis on process rather than outputs

approach is a more suitable approach than others in realising the desired outputs within the desired timeframe.

Table 1.2 illustrates some of the advantages and disadvantages of these three different approaches to managing change, noted by the Fellows.

Lessons learned

Perhaps the most useful 'non-traditional' tip not found in any of the standard texts on managing change was offered by one Fellow: 'Hold your nerve!' Seeing change through invariably gets tough. There were many points of agreement in terms of what worked well in launching and delivering projects. These are considered under three headings: the planning stage, actioning the change strategy, and monitoring and evaluation of the change.

The planning stage

At the commencement of the change initiative, Fellows were encouraged by the LFHE to adopt project management techniques. This was to ensure there was a basic framework which would better guarantee the achievement of the desired outcomes within the nine-month timeframe. All were encouraged to determine clear roles and responsibilities, particularly with respect to four roles: first, the project leader; second, the project manager; third, the project steering group; and, finally, the project team.

The *project leader*, or champion of the change, it was suggested, should be someone with sufficient status and clout to provide leadership and a strong level of confidence in both the vision and the rationale for the project. As 80 per cent of the LFFP Fellows were Senior Management Team (SMT) members, the role of leader clearly fell to them. It was emphasised that given the breadth and depth of their portfolios, it was unrealistic for them to manage the project as well.

The *project manager*, it was suggested, should, if possible, be a separate role. In over 90 per cent of the projects, the funding for the project was used to appoint a project manager (ranging from a third of their time to full time). This role was often filled by seconding of a member of staff, and 'back filling' the secondee's post, so as to develop and broaden the experience of two members of internal staff.

Additionally, it was recommended that these institutional change projects should have a *steering group* primarily responsible for the strategic planning of the project. Additionally, the role of the steering group was not only to provide support for the project leader and the manager, but also to provide a sense of collective responsibility. Diversity of membership would ensure that a range of perspectives could be taken into account when planning and monitoring the change. As part of this steering group, Fellows were encouraged by the LFHE to consider having someone external to the organisation as part of the steering group – be it someone who had introduced a similar initiative or change within their own institution, or someone with recognised expertise in the proposed area of change. A number of Fellows commented that having someone from outside the sector was a great benefit in terms of being regularly challenged and encouraged to think 'outside the box'.

Finally, the *project team* comprised those whose responsibility it was for the day-to-day delivery of the change, with the focus primarily on operational detail. Supported by the project leader, manager and steering group, and probably working to the broad parameters set by the former, the project team's responsibility was to action and monitor the delivery of the change. Where institutions had set up this infrastructure – i.e. project leader, project manager, steering group and project team – for delivery of their projects, it was noted that there was no confusion with respect to roles, responsibilities, and accountabilities within this 'hierarchy' and beyond. This led to a subsequent greater confidence with respect to both the rationale for change and the whole process. A process with which all were expected to engage.

A further key issue which must be addressed in the planning stage was achieving clarity about aims, ensuring that aims were (i) kept ambitious yet realistic, and (ii) simple and easy to remember, particularly for the benefit of staff asking 'what exactly are we trying to do here?' So often with change initiatives both leaders and followers lose sight of what the aims of the initiative are, primarily due to a failure to determine these in a simple, clear and concise sentence.

With respect to the scheduling of the change initiative – to include planning, roll out, monitoring and evaluation, many of the Fellows commented on what some perceived to be an almost disproportionate amount of time required at the planning stage. A number made statements such as 'Don't underestimate the amount of time or the volume of work involved', but also noting 'Planning [is] essential'. One would think that the latter comment was obvious. Far too often, however, in the haste to get on with a task, individuals feel compelled to launch into action without due regard to the planning process. Multi-layered planning can save so much time in the long run, particularly where contingency planning has been undertaken.

Actioning the change strategy

Leadership was deemed to be crucial, with a range of views as to its importance at different stages of the change. The fundamental purpose of leadership, further to providing a vision of what success further to the change would look like, is to deal with the dynamics of change. Bearing in mind the cultural anatomy (Figure 1.1), which will become affected by the change, a range of different forces will be unleashed over the course of the change transition, and these will have to be managed. Thus 'walking the talk' and visibility are crucial, keeping staff functioning at one level but hopefully at a higher level, and motivated, even during the lowest ebb of the process.

A clear set of values should underpin all messages. As Collins and Porras (1996) note, 'companies that endure success have a core purpose and core values that remain fixed while their strategies and practices endlessly adapt to a changing world' (p. 21). Values such as dignity at work, respect for individuals and their perspectives, listening more and talking less, are all values which should be role modelled by those leading and managing the change. As leaders 'walk this talk', such values should also serve to underpin all interactions.

All the Fellows recognised that the quality of personal relationships is essential (a manifestation of values), and that for the change to be successful, it had to be viewed as a joint effort, not a 'them and us'. By and large, leaders and staff see change differently. For leaders, change provides opportunities in terms of both the organisation and themselves. (How many staff have moved on to a more senior role further to leading or managing a significant change initiative?) But for many staff, change is perceived as disruptive and threatening (i.e. they see themselves as on the receiving end of relentless change which some cynically suggest is only to the benefit of those looking out for their next promotion). Strebel (1996) addresses this dichotomy by proposing a three-dimensional 'personal compact' – formal, psychological and social. The personal compact is achieved by the leader taking the initiative and providing the context for change. This is achieved by gaining personal commitments, articulating performance standards and gaining binding agreements. In this study, such a compact was achieved by techniques such as 'walking the talk', team working, focus groups, training and development.

Having an inclusive approach was another means of achieving the 'compact'. By this was meant adopting a consultative process to ensure that all staff feel that they have had an opportunity not only to engage with the vision but also to influence what their role might look like in this vision. An aid to inclusivity was having a project team to provide the openness, teamwork and support to allow for the 'tentacles' of the change to reach into all areas and for communication to be more personalised. Some noted, however, that where the change wasn't as successful as they might have hoped, it was due to the failure to anticipate the degree of training and development required.

Such teamwork was seen to have the additional benefit that 'working collaboratively helped overcome resistance'. This was deemed to be a great strength of the above approach and one that some institutions suggested was a key factor in their success.

Communication, along with car parking, must be one issue that everyone in every HE institution agrees is a major problem. Communication in the course of announcing and managing change is even more crucial, and therefore communication strategies should be carefully thought through and predetermined. A communication strategy should keep all stakeholders involved using a range of media, but, bearing in mind that to gain the confidence of those front line staff expected to deliver the change, nothing beats face-to-face communication. Sufficient account must be taken of providing opportunities to allow counter viewpoints to surface in order to challenge and persuade and such time should be scheduled and built into the communications strategy. Any communications strategy will recognise that regular (i.e. not just at the launch of a new initiative) face-to-face conversations are crucial and that good communication takes time. However, this appears to be the area that regularly gets squeezed, particularly when crisis management or other priorities suddenly take precedence. The majority of Fellows commented on the dangers of over-reliance on electronic communication.

Quick wins were seen as a means of boosting confidence, but it was also noted that *slow wins* were deemed to be more difficult to achieve but far more capable of making a significant impact. Thus Fellows saw the need to carefully balance pace and progress. Pace in progress was seen as a key responsibility of the leader and project manager, alongside watching out for any contingencies. As Webb (1994) noted over a decade ago when writing about change in HE, 'I am intrigued by the complex interaction of the planned and the serendipitous' (p. 43).

Monitoring and evaluation

Key lessons learned from the monitoring and evaluation stage focused on the need for an 'effective and controllable implementation plan' combined with 'clear evaluation measures', for, without these, there was no base line from which to gauge progress. Other lessons varied according to the underpinning philosophy of change management adopted by the Fellow. For example, in the structured framework approach, the difficulties of the 'transition cascade' were noted, along with the overall complexity of 'moving into the implementation phase'. Despite this approach leading to a clear plan and evaluation measures (with it being essentially a top-down approach), sometimes insufficient attention was paid to the various means and stages of gaining 'buy-in' from the staff whose commitment and efforts are necessary to deliver the change.

In the incentivised approach, the key difficulty was focused on the on-going time required for the project leader and project manager to ensure that proper support was provided for individuals engaged in the transition. Despite the incentives and the great will and motivation amongst those incentivised to change, to support them throughout the transition required more time than the project leaders and managers had anticipated and planned for. This difficulty strongly resonates with the work of Bridges (2005).

'Gaining buy-in' or 'leadership and management time' were not such an issue with the capacity building approach, which in essence is a concurrent 'top-down' (albeit often from one champion at the 'top' and as the LFFP Fellows were required to be either a member of the SMT or someone with the credibility to lead corporate change) and 'bottom-up' approach (albeit a select group of the converted). Unlike the previous two approaches, the difficulty of this approach was sometimes perceived to be the risk of marginalisation – i.e. being seen as a 'pet' project of one individual, aided by the zeal of others sharing a similar enthusiasm. Taking such an initiative forward to the point of embedding it was therefore more difficult. Some suggested that there were problems with, for example, 'not gaining 100 per cent support from [the] SMT'. Once again, this highlights the importance of the planning stage. Undertaking a risk assessment which includes stakeholder analysis could have revealed where the supporters might reside, but, more important in this case, where the resistors might lie. It is only when a multi-faceted and detailed mapping exercise is undertaken that the appropriate approach can be determined.

Conclusions

Whether it be in the private or public sector (or, the hybrid!), clearly successful change depends on individual people and their collective actions. Clear leadership, enacting trust in and respect for both individuals and teams, promotes a culture where people feel empowered to take on greater responsibility and deliver results. Through leading by example ('walking the talk', investing time in staff to cultivate constructive working relationships) the foundations for successful change management, implementation and embedding are paved. Increasingly, universities are recognising, like their counterparts in the private sector, that leadership *does* matter. It is only authentic leaders who are able to make the vision become a reality. This results from engaging followership, who, in turn, deliver meaningful and lasting change. This may, on occasions, require the additional unique piece of advice for leading and managing change coming out of this study – 'Hold your nerve!' I'm sure that, too, is no different in the private sector!

References

Boyatzis, R. and McKee, A. (2005) *Resonant Leadership*, HBS Press: Boston.

Bridges, W. (2005) *Managing Transitions* (2nd edn), Nicholas Brearley Publishing: London.

Bullock, R. and Batten, D. (1985) 'It's just a phase we're going through', *Group and Organization Studies*, Dec.

Collins, J. (2001) *Good to Great*, Random House: London.

Collins, J. and Porras, J. (1996) 'Building your company's vision', *Harvard Business Review*, Sept.–Oct.

Duck, J. (1993) 'Managing change: the art of balancing', *Harvard Business Review*, Nov.–Dec.

Johnson, G. and Scholes, K. (2005) *Exploring Corporate Strategy* (7th edn), Prentice Hall: Harlow.

Kanter, R., Stein, B. and Jick, T. (1992) *The Challenge of Organisational Change*, Free Press: New York.

Kotter, J. (1996) *Leading Change*, Harvard Business School Press: Boston.

Mintzberg, H. (1994) *The Rise and Fall of Strategic Planning*, Prentice Hall: Hemel Hempstead.

Nadler, D. and Tushman, M. (1997) *Competing by Design*, Oxford University Press: London.

Schein, E. (1992) *Organisational Culture and Leadership: A Dynamic View*, Jossey Bass: San Francisco.

Shattock, M. (2003) *Managing Successful Universities*, Society for Research into Higher Education, Oxford University Press: Maidenhead.

Slowey, M. (ed.) (1995) *Implementing Change From Within Universities and Colleges*, Kogan Page: London.

Strebel, P. (1996) 'Why do employees resist change?', *Harvard Business Review*, May–June.

Webb, A. (1994) 'Two tales from a reluctant manager' in S. Weil (ed.) *Introducing Change from the Top in Universities and Colleges*, Kogan Page: London.

Weil, S. (ed.) (1994) *Introducing Change from the Top in Universities and Colleges*, Kogan Page: London.

Part I

Structured frameworks for leading and managing change

Chapter 2

Management by processes and facts

Paul Evans

This chapter is concerned with how Liverpool John Moores University (LJMU) addressed the joint issues of aligning key business processes with the strategic plan and how such processes were subsequently developed and improved. Readers may wish to consider this chapter in the context of Chapter 4 on strategic planning. There is a leadership dilemma in all organisations that aspire to deliver consistent performance of processes across conventional organisational structures. This chapter describes how LJMU defined its process management framework in the context of strategy; how the concept of process ownership was used in an attempt to address the leadership dilemma; and how the principle of 'involving people' was applied to process review and improvement. It is a frank account of the successes and difficulties and provides useful lessons for any Higher Education Institution contemplating such a challenging but worthwhile project.

Context

LJMU committed to use the European Foundation for Quality Management (EFQM) *Excellence Model* (EFQM 2003a) as the basis for the development of its management system in 2002 (see Figure 2.1). A diagnostic self-assessment against that model was undertaken in early 2003 resulting in a programme of improvement projects. One of the most fundamental findings of this self-assessment was a clear lack of connection between the process of strategic planning and execution and the process management system required to deliver that strategy. It was also quite evident that there was limited consistency in the way in which key processes were understood and managed across the faculties and support services. In consequence, a major process framework project was put in place with the objectives of creating a strategic alignment of processes; of prioritising processes for bringing them under control; and of establishing a long-term cycle of review and improvement. Implied within this project was the need to assess process performance in future through objective and measurable criteria. There was some evidence to suggest that past decision making in relation to process improvement had

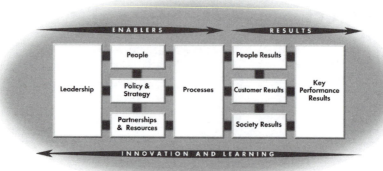

Figure 2.1 The EFQM Excellence Model.

® The EFQM *Excellence Model* is a registered trademark of EFQM

been based on anecdote. The University's intention was to improve this situation to allow 'Management by Processes and Fact': one of the fundamental concepts of excellence (EFQM 2003b).

The first steps

In common with other significant LJMU projects, the process framework project utilised an adaptation of the established public sector project management methodology, 'Prince2'. A project steering group was established and a project manager appointed. At the same time, the University's senior management engaged with a review of strategy in preparation for the publication of its strategic plan for the period from 2003 to 2008. This created an opportunity to ensure that the strategy was clearly defined in operational process terms.

Figure 2.2 illustrates the strategic process map on which the strategic plan was based. This shows the four core processes of the University, so defined to represent the core academic and student-related activity of LJMU as delivered by the faculties. At the top of the process map, management processes were defined, that is, those required to provide the overall management controls in support of the core activity, for example governance, finance and quality assurance. At the foot of the process map, infrastructure processes were defined, that is, those required to provide the necessary infrastructure to support the core activity, for example property, learning resources and ICT. Collectively, the processes shown in Figure 2.2 were referred to as the strategic processes.

Each strategic process was allocated a strategic process owner (SPO) who

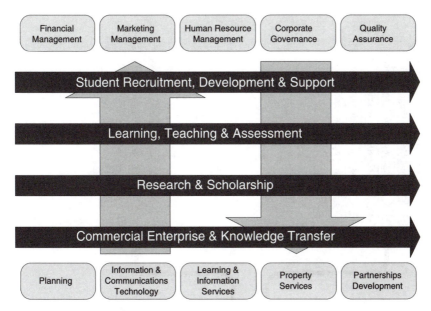

Figure 2.2 LJMU strategic process map.

© Liverpool John Moores University 2004

was a member of the LJMU senior management team, known as the strategic management group (SMG). Working with the project team, each SPO identified a number of key processes; effectively these were the sub-processes that contributed collectively to the delivery of the strategic processes. Once identified, these key processes were mapped under their respective strategic processes. Figure 2.3 shows an example of this mapping under each of the core strategic processes. Similar maps were produced for the management and infrastructure strategic processes.

Whilst SPOs were concerned with maintaining an oversight of the related key processes and prioritising these for review, day-to-day responsibility for the operation of these was allocated to key process owners (KPOs). These people were responsible for leading the reviews of their respective processes and the subsequent training and implementation plans. KPOs were unlikely to have full line-management responsibility for all staff who contributed to the delivery of their process. Most staff would continue to be managed locally, whilst in process management terms they would be required to conform to the defined process standards as set by the KPO. However, it was not the intention to impose rigid or inflexible processes. A process can be considered as a series of related and interdependent tasks. It was recognised very early that it would be necessary for staff in faculties to perform these tasks flexibly to suit local conditions. The standardisation of any process was

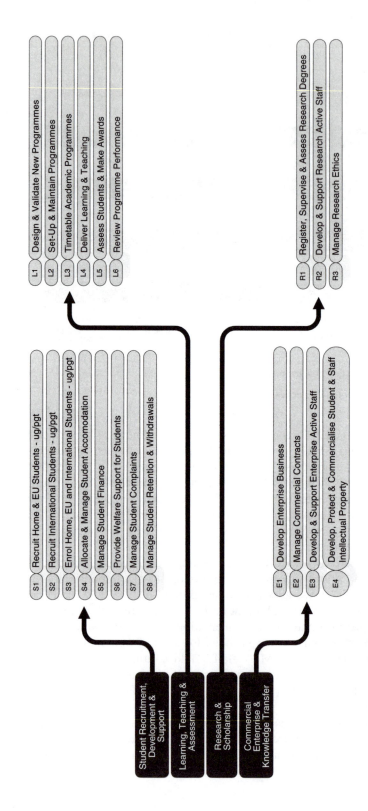

S1 Recruit Home & EU Students - ug/pgt
S2 Recruit International Students - ug/pgt
S3 Enrol Home, EU and International Students - ug/pgt
S4 Allocate & Manage Student Accomodation
S5 Manage Student Finance
S6 Provide Welfare Support for Students
S7 Manage Student Complaints
S8 Manage Student Retention & Withdrawals

L1 Design & Validate New Programmes
L2 Set-Up & Maintain Programmes
L3 Timetable Academic Programmes
L4 Deliver Learning & Teaching
L5 Assess Students & Make Awards
L6 Review Programme Performance

R1 Register, Supervise & Assess Research Degrees
R2 Develop & Support Research Active Staff
R3 Manage Research Ethics

E1 Develop Enterprise Business
E2 Manage Commercial Contracts
E3 Develop & Support Enterprise Active Staff
E4 Develop, Protect & Commercialise Student & Staff Intellectual Property

Student Recruitment, Development & Support

Learning, Teaching & Assessment

Research & Scholarship

Commercial Enterprise & Knowledge Transfer

Figure 2.3 LJMU core process map.

© Liverpool John Moores University 2004

therefore limited to ensuring that all of the tasks within the process were delivered to the same standard; for example, whilst the task could be carried out in a variety of ways in each faculty, it would have to work with standard inputs and produce standard outputs to standard timescales for the overall process to remain consistent and in control.

Key processes were prioritised for review on the following basis:

- processes that were 'mission critical'
- processes that were newly required by the strategy
- processes that were currently subject to different 'customs and practices' across faculties that might benefit from 'best-practice' treatment.

To give some examples, all processes that concerned the recruitment and enrolment of students were considered 'mission critical' and were prioritised for immediate review. A new process to standardise the means by which research active staff could be developed and supported arose directly from the 2003–8 strategic plan. This too was prioritised for early review to support a key strategic objective. A process relating to the registration, supervision and assessment of research students was carried out differently in each faculty. A review was prioritised here to identify and implement best practice across the University.

Project execution

Review methodology

The University gave careful consideration to the review methodology, specifically the composition and leadership of review teams; the timeframe for each review; documentation and expected outputs; and implementation.

With regard to the *composition and leadership* issue, this was a decision that had to be made in the context of the University's commitment to the fundamental concepts of excellence (EFQM 2003b). One such concept was 'people development and involvement'. The value of people involvement and empowerment has been well researched and Oakland and Oakland (2001) provides a useful start-point for those interested in the concept. Subsequently, Oakland (2005) has observed that 'better processes and full involvement of the people should be the focus for quality professionals in the 21st Century'.

From the beginning of its excellence programme, LJMU had approached the issue of people involvement by use of the 'diagonal slice' team; so named because it was composed of people drawn from across the University's functions, from all grades and from all levels of experience (noting that newer staff can bring different insights). The evidence gathering phase for the original EFQM self-assessment had been successfully conducted using a 'diagonal slice' so it was a logical progression for the University to adopt this approach for process review, with review teams being drawn from those functions who ran the process in question, or who were dependent on its outcomes. Team size varied between eight and fifteen people, depending on the scope and complexity of the process. When the upper limit was exceeded, team performance was compromised. Occasionally it was preferred to establish small teams on the understanding that some key stakeholders would be consulted as part of the review process, rather than have a full input.

The leadership issue was also carefully thought through. Whilst the key process owner would be a member of the review team and would have full responsibility for the implementation of the new or revised process, there was a concern that their leadership of the review process itself could be perceived as bringing some bias. In consequence, all reviews were facilitated by people independent from the process under review. Initially, there were issues about the release of staff from their normal duties to fulfil their review team roles. However, the University moved to establish that contribution to review and improvement activity is part of everyone's job and line managers were encouraged to allow time for such work. Key to this was to ensure widespread involvement of staff and to avoid overburdening the naturally enthusiastic, or to sidelining the 'usual suspects'; indeed the inclusion of 'devout sceptics' was found to be beneficial to the quality of the review and the implementation process.

The *timeframe* for each review was a particular concern to the SMG. Previously, improvement projects had been led by 'committee of inquiry' style project teams, often taking several months, or even years, to consult and seek approval through the labyrinth of committees. It was decided that a process review should be split into three phases, with timeframes specified appropriately:

- the *process review* phase: the period in which the 'diagonal slice' team works to produce recommendations for the new/revised process, and its implementation;
- the *process implementation* phase: the period in which the key process owner, supported by the 'diagonal slice' team communicates the new process, leads any structural changes required, arranges training for those affected and ensures that agreed documentation is in place;
- the *implementation review* phase: an appropriate point in the future, usually twelve months, to review the effectiveness of the implementation.

The timeframe for the *implementation* phase was to be determined by the process review. In many cases it would be necessary to position the implementation carefully to ensure that it did not disrupt the current cycle for that process. Also the extent of change proposed would influence the time needed for implementation. Likewise, the most useful time to assess effectiveness of the new process would be after it had run through at least one full cycle of operation. The timing would therefore be dependent on the implementation date. However, the review phase was set by the Vice-Chancellor to be a challenging timeframe of four to six weeks, depending on the size and complexity of the process in question.

It was recognised that the format and type of any documentation required to support the process would vary according to the type of process. For example, high volume transactional processes, such as recruitment and enrolment could be documented using flowcharts, supported by cross-reference to policy and procedural documents. For softer processes, such as the development and support of research active staff, flowcharts would be inappropriate, but could be documented in the form of guidance papers, cross-referencing to the support resources available. In consequence, the documentation requirements for each process review would be determined by the review itself. However, it was felt desirable that where flowcharts were to be used, these should adopt a university standard. Deployment (or responsibility) flowcharts were selected as they had the benefit of clearly defining the roles and responsibilities of individual departments, as well as the process interfaces between departments.

Each review project was planned on a bespoke basis with the strategic process owner, key process owner and facilitator meeting approximately four weeks before the expected project commencement date (see Table 2.1). The agenda for this meeting was to conduct an initial scoping of the process under review; from which the appropriate team composition could be determined. The expected timeframe, in the range four to six weeks, and schedule of meetings was also agreed. The SPO would then announce the process review through the University's intranet website, requesting volunteers. For the most part, demand for participation exceeded the number of places available; however, where there were shortfalls, either in total or from key functions, some direct approaches were made. Team members were then selected by the SPO and KPO on the basis of creating a balanced 'diagonal slice' made up of all grades, disciplines and experience levels.

Table 2.1 Implementation phase

Step 1	Determine the strategic process owner (SPO), key process owner (KPO) and facilitator
Step 2	Determine the size and complexity of the process
Step 3	Determine documentation requirements (e.g. flow charts, roles and responsibilities, departmental interfaces)
Step 4	Undertake initial scoping
Step 5	Determine expected timeframe and schedule of meetings
Step 6	SPO to announce the process review via the intranet website, requesting volunteers
Step 7	Recruitment to the team according to representative 'cross slice'

The process review phase

Having completed the planning and team selection phases, the 'diagonal slice' team meetings were convened. Each review followed one of two similarly structured formats, depending upon whether the process in question was new, or whether it was an existing process.

The first team meeting for each review was used to set the scene for the review and to outline the method to be followed. The first meeting was always scheduled to last three hours with the following typical agenda.

- *Team introductions* The meeting would open with an informal session where team members were asked to introduce themselves to each other and to state why they had volunteered for the review and what they hoped to gain personally from participation; and what they hoped for in terms of review outcomes.
- *Formal introduction* Following this, and usually undertaken by the strategic or key process owner, would be a formal introduction outlining the rationale for the review, the roles and responsibilities of the team and the means by which the recommendations would be approved and implemented.
- *Introduction to process management* The facilitator would then introduce the tools and techniques that would be used.
- *Establishment of key principles* The first facilitated session would be next, in which team members 'brainstormed' and agreed the principles on which an ideal version of the process in question would operate. Typically, this included such general statements as 'seamless' and 'no duplication', or process specific statements such as 'consistent data input' and 'one-stop-shop' for students.
- *Identifying influences and constraints* In this second facilitated session, the team identified existing policies that influenced the scope of the review. For example, student recruitment processes were influenced by admissions and widening participation policies. They would also consider any limitations on the scope of the review, for example, government policy or interfaces with external agencies (e.g. HEFCE, UCAS, etc.).
- *Agreeing review roles* Having established principles, influences and constraints, the team would then commit to the remaining dates of the review phase, to the undertaking of any agreed tasks between meetings and to consult with their immediate colleagues between meetings and feed this back in the review.
- *Mapping the existing process* If the process was already in place, the team then attempted to map its current operation. This third facilitated session was an active 'on-the-feet' task involving all of the team using 'post-it' notes to capture the existing tasks, responsible departments and individuals. The approach could be used for processes that were not suited

to the use of flowcharts. The team were asked to critique the existing process in the context of the principles that they had previously defined. This phase would often highlight non-adherence to these principles, significant duplication and high levels of complexity. Finishing the first meeting on such a note was designed to emphasise the need for the review and to assist the team in convincing colleagues of this fact. No process was deemed to be fully fit for purpose at this stage.

For the second meeting, usually one week later and of two hours duration, team members would return with the results of any agreed actions and consultation and the facilitator would recap the outcomes of the opening meeting, having previously circulated these by e-mail. The full meeting would be taken up by the team establishing a process that met all the principles agreed at the first meeting. This would then be captured in the form of a deployment flowchart, or as an outline sketch for a guidance or procedural document. Depending on the size and complexity of the process, this step sometimes required up to two further meetings. In the case of new processes, this was also started at the second meeting, having concluded the first meeting with the 'agreeing review roles' step.

The final two meetings involved the refinement of the outline process through testing the concept with colleagues in between and the agreement of the recommendations to be put to the SMG, including the outline implementation plan.

The process implementation phase

In the period immediately following the review phase, the SPO and KPO would meet to confirm the final recommendations and the implementation plan. This discussion would include any organisational implications, such as changes of structure or reporting lines. An output from this meeting would be a final report that would then be presented to the SMG for approval and good practice was for this to be seen and commented on by the review team before submission.

On approval, the KPO would lead the implementation project. This would include communicating the new process to all involved parties and ensuring that appropriate training was given. Whilst the implementation plan would be tailored to specific process reviews, a key principle was that communication and training preceded the final implementation date. Any structural or line reporting changes would be made at this point.

The implementation review stage

As stated previously, a further review of the implementation and the effectiveness of the new or revised process would be undertaken at the end of a full cycle. At the time of writing, the several reviews completed under this project to date were becoming due for such reflection but these had not yet been completed. The pilot review, student enrolment, was further reviewed in the summer of 2005 and the successful implementation of arrangements for new students was subsequently extended to include returning students. However, as can be seen later under 'lessons learned', the process review project revealed fundamental structural issues in relation those processes relating to all aspects of 'student administration'. In consequence, such processes would need to be reviewed further once those issues had been resolved.

Lessons learned

Any project that sets out to review the very heart of how a university operates is by definition a challenge. The process framework project at LJMU is living proof of this statement, and in starting out on a long-term commitment to management by processes and facts, the University has already made significant and successful improvements to several key processes. However, whilst these successes may be welcome, LJMU has also learned many useful lessons that are now being built in to the next planned series of reviews.

What went well

In terms of the University's first self-assessment using the EFQM Excellence Model, the project has already addressed the issue of aligning key business processes with the strategic plan, and has made significant inroads into how such processes are subsequently developed and improved. The process framework and structure has helped the University come to terms with managing complexity and to focus more on what is important to delivering strategy. The review methodology has been broadly successful in delivering robust process improvement proposals by encouraging objective analysis and decision making against defined success criteria. The University's second *Excellence Model* Self-Assessment, conducted in late 2005 and which included external assessors, reported positively on progress made.

One of the most successful aspects of the project was the concept of the 'diagonal slice' team. There was positive feedback from participants in terms of their involvement and it was not difficult to obtain the right numbers and balance of volunteers. Throughout the review phase there was a genuine commitment amongst team members to create efficient and value-adding processes. There was also very little evidence of self-interest or protectionism. The concept of the 'diagonal slice' has started to become embedded within the culture of LJMU and has been extended to other projects looking at specific improvement requirements, including root-and-branch reviews of the property services and student administration functions.

Another success has been the extent to which it has been possible for

LJMU to secure the long-term commitment of SMG to the process framework and its development.

What went less well

Whilst the review phases of all projects reached successful conclusions, there was significant variability in the implementation phase. In some cases, implementation plans were not as robust as they should have been and key aspects of communication and training were not identified or planned. This led to problems later in the implementation process, particularly in terms of understanding and acceptance from the majority of staff who were non-participants. A further cause of this lack of acceptance was identified as being rooted in a failure by some review phase participants to consult adequately with their colleagues as the review progressed. In consequence, the 'not-invented-here' syndrome became a barrier to implementation. Another barrier could be described as the 'special-case' syndrome, where individual departments claimed that the new process did not fit with their needs or ways of working. Whilst there was an expressed will for more standardised ways of doing things, the extent to which some process tasks were dispersed to a large number of individual units (particularly the student administration processes) was mitigating against this will.

These barriers also tested the project management skills of the key process owners, highlighting that the University had not done enough to develop these people in this role. Similarly, the level to which strategic process owners engaged in practice, particularly at the implementation phase, was variable. The most successful projects shared a common feature of strong leadership by both KPOs and SPOs at all stages of the review.

In consequence, three key lessons were learned:

- the need to ensure consistent behaviours by KPOs and SPOs and to have their responsibilities clearly defined;
- the need to identify project management skills gaps and to provide appropriate training;
- the need to ensure communication between participants and non-participants at all stages.

A fourth and more fundamental lesson came from the implementation problems associated with the most complex processes, mainly those associated with student administration. The vast variation in practice across as many as 30 individual local administration offices and the complex layers of administration between central teams, campus centres, faculties and school offices, suggested that there were structural issues that no single process review could address. The conclusion that LJMU drew from this was that the student administration structure had developed through successive organisational changes to a point where it was overly complicated for its users – both students and academic staff. It needed to be reviewed and the several individual processes that collectively sat within this broad function needed to be further reviewed on completion of the structural review. A diagonal slice team was established for this purpose and, at the time of writing, a more coherent structure through which standardised processes can operate was being proposed for implementation. Further process reviews are planned.

Summary

The process framework project at LJMU is a long-term commitment. Despite many difficulties its value is understood and appreciated. Key lessons have been learned and are being addressed as part of this long-term commitment. It has become clear at LJMU that the establishment of a process framework connected to strategy is a useful means to manage complexity, and universities are complex organisations indeed. It has also shown that taking on a project to improve operations in the 'bite-size chunks' of individual processes can be both challenging and rewarding and that by doing so, in a structured and coordinated way, more fundamental issues can be identified and addressed.

Process review and improvement is becoming the accepted way of life at LJMU. The following opinion is not untypical.

> This process (of review) has been critical in getting a diverse set of service and academic interests together to streamline key university processes.
> (Professor Paulo Lisboa, Head of Graduate School)

References

European Foundation for Quality Management (EFQM) (2003a) *The EFQM Excellence Model*, European Foundation for Quality Management: Brussels (www.efqm.org).

European Foundation for Quality Management (EFQM) (2003b) *The Fundamental Concepts of Excellence*, European Foundation for Quality Management: Brussels (www.efqm.org).

Oakland, S. and Oakland, J. S. (2001) 'Current people management issues in world-class organizations', *Total Quality Management*, 12(6): 773–88.

Oakland, J. S. (2005) 'From quality to excellence in the twenty-first century', *Total Quality Management and Business Excellence*, 16(8/9): 1503–1060.

Chapter 3

Conversational, not confrontational

A new approach to quality

Bob Munn

This chapter describes how a new 'right-touch' quality framework for the University of Manchester was shaped. The new framework was needed because the University itself was newly formed. A conversational approach designed to reflect how the new framework would operate was adopted whereby every school in the University was visited and staff were invited to express their hopes and fears for the new framework. This time-consuming process revealed hopes for simplicity, clarity and efficiency, and fears that rigour might be lost. This emergent approach helped to shape the new framework and to develop trust in the plans.

A new start

The new University of Manchester was formed on 1 October 2004 from UMIST (the University of Manchester Institute of Science and Technology) and the Victoria University of Manchester. The ambition was to make the new university more than just the sum of its parts through a 'step change', guided by a determination to accept nothing from its precursor universities that did not represent best practice.

Among the many areas for attention was the quality framework, where the aim was to introduce new 'right-touch' procedures rather than what had often been seen as effective but burdensome and bureaucratic ones in the precursor universities. Guiding principles also emerged from goals asserted in the University's strategic plan, *Towards Manchester 2015*: excellent teaching and learning; a collegial culture; and efficient, effective management. Externally, the Quality Assurance Agency for Higher Education had been modifying its methodology, focusing its audits on institutions' own self-evaluation and reporting processes. In this context, there was an opportunity to operate quality processes that were less process-oriented and rigid than previously, but no less thorough.

A 'right-touch' approach is one that is fit for purpose, being restricted to what is necessary, with an intensity commensurate to the risk and appropriate to the circumstances. Review can then be proportional, evaluative and predictive, focusing on areas for attention and so reducing the time and energy required. It enhances academic quality by sharing strengths and addressing weaknesses, whereas a 'heavy' prescriptive approach risks distracting time and attention away from the key issues. In this way the goals of excellent teaching and learning and efficient, effective management can both be met. A 'right-touch' is also distinguishable from a 'light-touch' approach. A light touch reduces regulation, but may remain unselective, and may become confused with a 'soft touch' that is too lenient, with insubstantial procedures that will not achieve the intended outcomes.

Preliminary work on the quality framework began when a team of academic and administrative staff attended the first Change Academy run by the Leadership Foundation for Higher Education (LFHE) and the Higher Education Academy (HEA) in September 2004. This four-day event allowed participating teams to work in a supported environment on a project to effect transformational change, in this case entitled *Joined-up working in learning, teaching and assessment*. This provided the opportunity to work on finalising the University's quality framework. Instead, however, the team ended up by developing a set of underlying principles against which to judge the appropriateness of the new processes (see Box 3.1). These principles were then used as a foundation in devising the operation of the quality framework.

The approach

Creating a new university by merging two universities is a major change in itself, but other major changes are nested within it. In the present instance, the new quality framework was required to constitute best practice, which might have to be invented rather than adapted. Teaching and learning pervade academic life even in a research-intensive university, and so the new framework would directly affect all academic staff. At the same time, academic staff from the two precursor universities would be carrying with them different prior experiences of quality processes. They would have different expectations – positive and negative – of the new ones, which would need their active engagement to work properly. It was therefore thought desirable to explore with staff their hopes and fears about the quality framework, and by so doing not only to acknowledge them but also to seek to address them in developing the framework.

Emergent methodologies are regularly applied across the social sciences. Although systematic, such approaches are non-directive, allowing the subjects to provide information according to their own needs and concerns. Reflection on and discussion of first-hand experiences can help people to manage their circumstances better through an enhanced understanding of the issues involved: simply being listened to is often empowering (Nichols 1995). In addition, the themes that emerge most recurrently from discussion reveal key issues to be addressed.

Box 3.1 Principles of the quality framework

1 The University is responsible for its awards and hence requires a framework for review and approval processes that lead to enhancement and feed into the planning of teaching and learning.
2 We assume that, as professionals, staff want to improve the experience for both teachers and learners.
3 We recognise that staff are also subject to other pressures, including research and the requirements of professional bodies.
4 We assume that staff will provide honest evaluations based on evidence that gives the full picture, good and bad.
5 Mistakes are serious only if you fail to learn from them.
6 Processes should be based on peer review that treats the University as a learning organisation and is supported by training, briefing and de-briefing.
7 Processes should be collective, reflective and respectful, not confrontational; they are based on dialogue, listening and support, not paperwork, policing and punishment.
8 Processes should be clear but flexible within set boundaries.
9 Processes should be focused and efficient, using a given process and information set for more than one purpose wherever possible.
10 Outcomes should emphasise achievement and should be disseminated as narratives as well as judgements.

Because of these advantages, a qualitative, emergent approach was thought suitable in seeking a deeper understanding of the situation. A conversational approach meant engaging in an exchange of thoughts, experiences and stories in a climate of mutual cooperation, so reflecting the University's goal of empowering collegiality. The value of conversational approaches to change has been argued by Shaw (2002).

The process

The project to develop the new quality framework was conducted by a team of three people: the Vice-President for Teaching and Learning as leader, the Head of Academic Quality, and a Project Officer recruited specifically. Development and evaluation were assisted by an Associate allocated by the Leadership Foundation, a specialist in strategic management and the management of innovation. The project lasted about six months.

Within a framework set by the University, operational responsibility for quality is devolved to the four Faculties and 23 Schools. Hence the team initially met each of the four Faculties. It then met all separate Schools, and finally Faculties again to report the emerging findings. At each meeting participants were invited to discuss their hopes and fears for the new quality framework and their intentions within it. An open agenda and open-ended questions were designed to promote dialogue and to exemplify the non-confrontational approach planned for the new framework: in McLuhan's (1964: 7) words, the medium is the message. It was hoped to start to embed the new processes through these conversations, and to update participants on developments where appropriate.

Conversation is distinguished by exchange of ideas, open-minded enquiry and cooperation. It is easier in relatively small groups of people when those conversing feel comfortable and 'at home', and so all meetings were organised in the Faculty or School concerned, with good-quality refreshments. Overall, 30 meetings were held, each lasting about an hour and a half, involving 134 participants in all.

Throughout each meeting, the Project Officer kept detailed notes focusing on content words carrying essential meaning and including direct quotations. Later, using a technique employed in grounded theory, the notes were organised into themes that had emerged, and a report was produced based on these themes. Meeting reports were sent to participants to correct or clarify if they wished, so that their intended meanings and messages were not distorted nor interpretations imposed on them. In practice, only six participants sent post-meeting comments; the reports were amended accordingly. Three participants also sent feedback after the meetings, with any comments being added to the information base. Reports and the raw notes remained confidential between the project team and the Schools. The notes were also analysed to confirm that the proceedings showed features characteristic of conversations, such as turn-taking with 'turns' of broadly comparable length.

At the time of the project, much other work was going on to establish the structures and processes in the new University, and an initial problem was that Heads of Schools declined a visit from the project because they felt overwhelmed by all the different people wanting to visit them. This was overcome by confirming that Heads themselves need not attend, but nevertheless several did. Some Faculties did not feel entirely comfortable about people from 'the Centre' visiting Schools without a Faculty presence, and suggested that their Schools should take part in a single visit together. A single Faculty visit was ruled out as being incompatible with the conversational approach, but it was agreed that Faculties could send a representative to visits to individual Schools if they chose and if the Schools in question agreed. As a result, three meetings with Schools in one Faculty were attended by a Faculty officer responsible for quality assurance and enhancement.

Hopes and fears

Influence of past experiences

Past experiences of quality processes naturally informed the hopes and fears that emerged from the conversational meetings. People hoped to see their positive experiences accentuated and their negative ones eliminated, although they did not always agree about what was positive or negative. In particular, some indignantly rejected the implication in the title of the project that past approaches to quality might have been confrontational. However, some of these people were identified by others with precisely the sort of confrontational approach that they hoped to see eliminated in the new processes.

Many Schools brought together groups of staff from both the precursor universities, with their different quality systems. Meanwhile, at the time of the meetings in the first half of 2005 the new university had yet to admit its own undergraduates (which did not happen until September 2005) and so was operating with an interim quality framework. Hence the views that emerged during the conversations were coloured by diverse previous and current experiences.

Staff accounts of past experiences generally indicated a desire for change. Processes were repeatedly described as 'burdensome', 'onerous' or 'cumbersome'. Former processes were needlessly 'elaborate' and featured 'gold plating', a phrase echoing that used in a recent review of the quality assurance framework in England to describe non-strategic and excessive responses to external review adopted by some institutions (Higher Education Funding Council for England 2005: paragraph 23). Nevertheless, it was recognised that there did need to be quality systems: 'There has got to be something in place for students and staff.' Moreover, not all views expressed about past academic quality procedures were negative, and there was little suggestion that former processes were entirely bad. 'People were honest and we did learn from one another.' Some Schools had found the processes undertaken in preparation for the merger positive and enhancing: 'opportunities for learning, and helpful'.

Schools were unanimous in finding former systems challenging to administer in one or more key aspects. Most commonly these challenges were the large amount of paperwork elicited by quality processes; the amount of time spent on them; and the restrictive nature of the procedures for reviews. On the matter of paperwork resulting from past review processes, feelings ran high. Documents prepared for programme approval processes and especially for reviews were described as 'wads', 'reams and reams', 'boxes and boxes', 'shelves full', 'suitcases full' of papers, 'a pile of papers that thick', 'a paper trail', 'a whole room set aside for paperwork' and even 'roomfuls'. One peer reviewer in the five-year process said, 'I was amazed by the amount of paperwork I was sent. I couldn't even carry [it].'

One Faculty had used the flexibility already available to make its contributions to the interim quality processes more like those foreshadowed for the new quality framework. This gave some staff a chance to reflect on the operation of these processes. Responses to this approach, though mixed, were broadly positive in tone. One School was unreservedly affirmative, finding the new approach 'more straightforward', less burdensome and less confrontational than former processes. Others found it 'a step in the right direction,' welcoming the oral, narrative format and the greater degree of reflection that the new approach encouraged: 'It reduced administration and entailed some real analysis of what we have done so far.' However, Schools also found too much detail to cover, and some found the new process more time-consuming than before.

A number of hopes and fears were articulated in the course of the discussions (see Box 3.2), and these are considered below.

Reduce bureaucracy

Not surprisingly, then, the strongest theme to emerge in connection with the new quality framework was a hope for more straightforward and less bureaucratic review processes: 'I think most of us hope that the old system will be replaced by one that is less cumbersome, prescriptive and bureaucratic.' Guidelines should be less directive and less concerned with 'tedious detail', creating 'a system that fits the purpose' and allows staff to focus on 'real-world' tasks. In general, procedures needed to be 'lean yet effective'. Rationalised processes were also recognised as important in securing staff acceptance of the quality framework where there was 'resistance and the need for people to change and trust [to be] gained'.

Box 3.2 The 'right touch' approach

1   Reduce bureaucracy
2   Rationalise paperwork
3   Provide clarity with flexibility
4   Focus on development
5   Operate processes quickly
6   Favour narrative over statistics
7   Avoid previous burdens
8   Maintain rigour.

Rationalise paperwork

The second strongest theme was a hope that the paperwork required for quality processes would be rationalised. 'I hope [the review] is done in a lighter way', with 'less to wade through'. There were positive reactions to plans for the new monitoring and review processes to accept documentation produced throughout the academic year, whether for internal use or for external review, rather than requiring the same information to be rewritten in a different format. 'That would be helpful and a great signal.' About half the Schools said that joint reviews between professional, statutory and regulatory bodies and the University could be a positive step. Positive reactions to joint reviews were strongest in the faculties where external scrutiny is most demanding, although they recognised that the prerequisites of some external bodies might differ too much from internal requirements for this to be practicable.

Provide clarity with flexibility

Other hopes were for clear, flexible and developmental processes. Ten of the Schools wanted clear and unambiguous guidelines for reviews. 'We are all drowning, so we need clear, easy words to understand.' 'We hope for a clarity of aims. What is it all for?' Many Schools wanted to 'domesticate' processes to accommodate their individual circumstances: 'I would very much like to see control [being] local to the School with as little interference as possible, as people outside the School have no knowledge of our circumstances.' The phrase 'one size does not fit all' came up more than once. 'We need flexible thinking to release energy and efficiency.' One School remarked that, given more ownership of processes by Schools, 'enthusiasm may increase'.

Focus on development

The need for reviews to be predictive as well as retrospective was stressed: '[Monitoring] should look forward, not just be a process of policing.' Over a third of the Schools hoped for greater opportunities for disseminating information, good practice and innovation amongst Schools and Faculties, 'to capture good practice across the University', and to avoid 're-inventing the wheel' by developing systems already used successfully elsewhere. The need for equilibrium between a simple system and an adequately thorough one was also raised: 'We need a balance between being as straightforward as possible while at the same time being rigorous.'

Operate processes quickly

Moving to hopes for future quality processes, these often originated in dissatisfaction with past ones. Over a third of the Schools hoped that processes involving external examiners would be made faster, with the forms rational-ised and with clearer guidelines. Over a quarter of the Schools wanted processes for programme approval that were as quick and uncomplicated as possible, with the autonomy to make minor changes without having to go through the full process required for a whole new programme.

Favour narrative over statistics

Over a quarter of the Schools welcomed an oral, narrative approach to annual reviews, with less focus on statistics. '*[If] we are asked to be more qualitative, more narrative, discussing [with] less analysing of quantitative data and numbers and a more descriptive and formative process, I think it's better.*' One School would prefer a '*conversational approach*', and another liked '*the idea of a narrative, conversational approach*', indicating that the approach to the new system was being effective. Prevailing frustration with the supply and reliability of student data from the Centre related to hopes for – and occasional cynicism about – the future. 'We cannot rely on the student system. I hope in the long term it won't be as horrific.' 'When I take the time to send the correct data, they ignore them,' said a Head of School. 'That's even if I do the bloody job myself!'

Avoid previous burdens

Perhaps encouragingly, comments about the future quality framework were expressed as hopes more than as fears, and the most commonly conveyed fears for new processes were the obverse of the hopes. The main concerns were that the negative elements of past processes would continue into the future. As one programme director admitted, 'I think my fears are con-ditioned by past experiences', and according to another, 'I am worried it will not be a light touch but that we will get bogged down with paperwork'. There was some anxiety that Faculties would add requirements to those from the Centre, so increasing the burden of processes, perhaps as another legacy of previous highly-structured approaches.

Maintain rigour

Not all the fears were the obverse of hopes. One fear mentioned by nearly a quarter of Schools was whether procedures developed for internal purposes would be sufficiently rigorous to satisfy external scrutiny. 'Can we say this will satisfy the QAA?' Schools were keen to establish that quality processes would remain robust: 'We want something rigorous, as people may think that a light touch means no touch.' 'I think there is a danger ... that conversational becomes too comfortable and nice, not recognizing what is weak.'

Maintain consistency

Some Schools saw a risk that flexibility could mean that processes would not be applied consistently. 'How can we ensure consistency and equity of treatment across four Faculties?' To counterbalance these risks, 'a firm sense of direction' from the Centre was needed. This fear apparently reflects the feeling that Schools sometimes feel disconnected from other Schools and Faculties, with too little flow of information.

Finally, given all the changes they had been going through, about a quarter of the Schools referred to fears of continuing change in some form.

Outcomes

The project showed the importance of preparation and information so that people fully understood the process and its intended outcomes. Recording, analysing and interpreting proceedings proved to be a major task for the Project Officer. All the conversational meetings took up considerable time, but they provided rich qualitative information that would have been hard to capture otherwise. Lessons learned are summarised in Box 3.3.

As a result of enquiring into Schools' hopes and fears for the new quality framework, the project was able to confirm some provisional decisions and interim processes and change others. The meetings additionally served to inform people and to let them raise issues about matters in the broader area of teaching, learning and assessment. In many cases, it proved possible to take action on these issues (for example, changes to the administration of the external examiner system), thereby demonstrating to participants that a conversational approach was effective in bringing about change.

A positive external view of the outcomes was provided in November 2005, when the University was subject to Institutional Audit by the Quality Assurance Agency for Higher Education. The quality framework was subjected to close attention, but was of course at an early stage of implementation. Noting this, the audit team nevertheless commented that the procedure for periodic review was founded on good practice and had the potential to

---

Box 3.3 Lessons learned

1 Prepare
2 Provide information – primarily the intended outcomes and the process
3 Organise meetings
4 Listen!
5 Record in order to analyse and interpret proceedings.

be effective and the procedure for annual monitoring had the potential to be very effective overall (Quality Assurance Agency for Higher Education 2005, paragraphs 177 and 178). The team also concluded that although the University was still going through a period of rapid change, it was handling the development of its own structures, policies and procedures appropriately (Quality Assurance Agency for Higher Education 2005, paragraph 183).

Conclusions

Good conversation develops when participants feel relaxed, at home and cared for. Conversations then help to develop trust, which cannot be asserted but must always be earned. Under these conditions, this approach could apply to other change projects. However, a project like this must explicitly intend to learn from people in order to help shape the change and not merely to communicate in order to sell the change.

For the members of the project team, conducting the project raised the profile of conversation as a change process. The following quotation, found in a book towards the end of the project, summarises very well the intentions of the project and, to a significant extent, describes its outcomes.

> Conversation is a meeting of minds with different memories and habits. When minds meet, they don't just exchange facts: they transform them, reshape them, draw different implications from them, engage in new trains of thought. Conversation doesn't just reshuffle the cards; it creates new cards.
>
> (Zeldin 1998: 14).

Overview

The conversational approach adopted in this project gathered information on people's hopes and fears for the new quality framework. It generally proved effective as a means of confirming interim elements of the framework and shaping it for roll-out. Informed by this approach, the final framework should be better adapted to the University's needs, being flexible rather than bureaucratic, more outcomes-oriented, and appropriate for both internal and external requirements. Such an approach would not necessarily be suitable where specific decisions need to be taken or a consensus reached, but it is suitable for enquiry and evaluation of ideas. It can also help to build trust by providing a mechanism for ancillary issues to be raised and attended to during the process.

References

Higher Education Funding Council for England (2005) *Publication 2005/35. Review of the Quality Assurance Framework: Phase one outcomes*, HEFCE: London.

McLuhan, H. M. (1964) *Understanding Media: The Extensions of Man*, McGraw Hill: New York.

Nichols, M. P. (1995) *The Lost Art of Listening*, The Guilford Press: New York.

Quality Assurance Agency for Higher Education (2005) *Institutional Audit Report RG210 11/05* (ISBN 1 84482 461 6); http://www.qaa.ac.uk/reviews/reports/institutional/manchester06/RG210UniversityofManchester.pdf.

Shaw, P. (2002) *Changing Conversations in Organizations: A Complexity Approach to Change*, Routledge: London.

Zeldin, T. (1998) *Conversation*, Harvill: London.

Chapter 4

Leadership and strategy

Simon Donoghue

Introduction

This chapter is concerned with how the University of Leeds (UofL) addressed the development of its corporate strategy using the 'balanced scorecard' and 'strategy map' approach. The chapter illustrates the import-ance of developing a strategy execution capability; most corporate strategies are valid but very rarely implemented. Yet the majority of the time which most organisations invest in strategy is around the strategy development pro-cess. The approach developed at UofL responds to this challenge, balancing the importance of the content of strategy and the capability to execute it. The chapter illustrates the relationship between the two activities, demonstrating the importance of strategy development being undertaken in a way that responds to the execution challenge. The project at the University of Leeds was path-finding in nature, and therefore should have a number of interesting learning points for other HE leaders and organisations. In particular, the chapter highlights the importance of the adoption of the 'balanced score-card' and 'strategy map' approach being undertaken in an evolutionary manner, providing time for the necessary learning and adaptation to take place. The chapter illustrates the leadership challenge.

The parallel development of strategy content and process is dependent upon leadership – but also has a considerable effect upon leadership devel-opment through focusing leadership around a key organisational task. At the time this chapter was written, UofL was at the end of the second year of this project. It is anticipated that it will take three to five years to fully embed the strategic management framework and demonstrate improved performance.

Background and context

September 2003 marked a turning point for the University of Leeds after several years of a successful strategy of expansion and growth under the leadership of Sir Professor Alan Wilson. The appointment of a new Vice-Chancellor, Professor Michael Arthur, introduced a renewed sense of aspiration, direction and purpose to the University. At that time the University faced considerable choices and challenges and it was apparent that in order to strengthen and secure its position in a leading position in UK and world HE, the University needed to define a new strategy. Developing strategic plans was not a new competence for the University. The University had developed strategies for HEFCE every five years and used these as a framework to guide and coordinate planning decisions, along with all other UK HE institutions.

The expectations placed upon the strategy process were, however, considerably different. The University had recognised the long-term importance of securing a UK and world leading competitive position, requiring a considerable and coordinated programme of strategic development. Hence, the effectiveness of this process would be judged upon its ability to deliver change, rather than simply providing a coordinated planning framework. It is widely recognised that most large organisations struggle effectively to implement strategy (Bridges 2005). Since strategy development and implementation was so critical to the long-term position of the University of Leeds, a project was established to ensure its effective development. The University also very importantly developed a new approach to managing, governing and implementing strategy.

The balanced scorecard/strategy map approach

The University of Leeds (UofL) made an early decision to adopt the 'strategy map' and 'balanced scorecard' approach for this strategic management framework (see Figure 4.1).

The adoption of this approach was based upon its strength in 'strategy execution' and the large number of complex organisations reporting successes in this regard. The foundations of the 'balanced scorecard' and its application are well documented – with several texts providing a comprehensive overview (Kaplan and Norton 2001, Kaplan and Norton 2004, Niven 2003). The initial research undertaken at UofL revealed limited evidence of the approach being used with HE. The 'balanced scorecard' framework adopted by UofL was designed to provide a way of describing, measuring and managing the strategy. The approach was based upon a body of knowledge developed by the 'balanced scorecard' collaborative gained from working with a number of companies through their 'hall of fame programme'. At the centre of this model are five basic principles of a 'strategy-focused' organisation:

1   *Mobilise change through executive leadership* ensuring that the project had top leadership sponsorship, further to working with the senior management of the University to define a long-term change agenda – articulated through a vision and strategy.

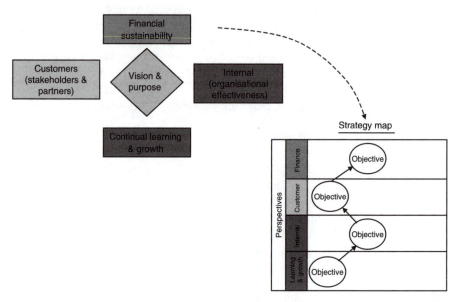

Figure 4.1 Balanced scorecard framework: four perspectives.

Source: Based upon work in Kaplan and Norton 2004

2   *Translate the strategy to operational terms* this part of the project was concerned with the development of a 'strategy map' supported by a 'balanced scorecard', supported by a number of key initiatives to deliver the key strategic priorities.

3   *Align the organisation to the strategy* alignment is a key part of the implementation challenge, concerning the process of effectively cascading the strategy throughout the University.

4   *Motivate to make strategy everyone's job* this part of the project was concerned with ensuring that the strategy connected with the entire University through effective communication and objective setting.

5   *Govern to make strategy a continual process* the final element of the approach was about ensuring that the strategy was integrated into the governance of the University, establishing regular reviews and reporting processes to ensure ongoing focus upon the strategy.

These basic principles provided the high level overview of the priorities for the project. During the early stages of development, considerable work was put into educating and communicating the importance of the overall framework, as there was a tendency for the 'performance measurement' aspects to dominate the strategic agenda. This was a particular challenge, as the culture of the organisation would have not responded to the framework being predominately measures-driven.

Project team

The strategy project was established by UofL strategy group, with the strategy group providing the sponsorship and leadership for the development of a strategy framework. The strategy group consisted of the University's senior management team and faculty Deans. In addition to this group, a high-level small multi-functional team was established to deliver the project, drawing in strong credible professional expertise from finance, planning, project management and development. The team did not have any considerable 'balanced scorecard'/'strategy map' exposure or experience. This experience was introduced into the University through a short intervention from external consultants, who provided initial facilitation and direction and transferred 'balanced scorecard' and 'strategy map' skills into the core team. During the first phase the project team facilitated the development and cascade of the 'strategy map' and associated processes across the institution. *Skills development and transfer* is a key consideration in any such project. The ability to cascade an effective framework and make it meaningful is linked to the University's ability to transfer skills from within a central project team into the wider organisation.

Strategy development

This section provides a case study overview structured around the ideas, approach and challenges faced in developing a strategic management framework based upon the five principles of a strategy-focused organisation. The narrative focuses upon some of the key decisions taken and on the challenges, rather than on providing a comprehensive overview of every element of the implementation. This helps the reader to consider how these principles apply within a modern large University environment.

Mobilise change through executive leadership

The initial stage of the project involved building a strong consensus amongst the senior managers of the University for the case for change. The new Vice-Chancellor was uniquely positioned to lead this stage, being in a position to challenge the University's view of its future direction. The Vice-Chancellor spearheaded this internal conversation, opening up a dialogue with staff across the University about the issues and priorities. This process ran for around two to three months, and was focused through a series of strategy group away-days, where the views and perspectives of members of staff were used to shape the new strategy. The debate was positioned around the University's vision and level of aspiration, exploring the concept of what the University future position should be (world-class) and how this could be achieved. As part of this process, a more open style of communication was established with the leadership of the University, providing managers of schools, services and departments with the opportunity to have a voice in the strategy. This was an essential early foundation in developing commitment around the new vision.

Strategy away-days provided the focus for the development stage of the strategy, but perhaps more importantly enabled the Vice-Chancellor to develop the engagement and commitment in the new strategy. This was a key stage in getting the quality of direction essential to effective implementation.

Leadership was a key component of the project and the successful implementation of the strategy. The relationship between the central project team role and the devolved responsibilities and accountabilities of leaders had to be continually balanced. This was difficult to achieve in practice, as there was an inevitable tendency for leaders and managers to concentrate their time on day-to-day activities and business as usual rather than engaging with the complexity of the 'strategy map' process. This was recognised as a risk in the very early stages and significant development work and support was put in place to help leaders to create time to consider strategy. There was very little point in the organisation creating a strategy at a pace that the organisational leadership could not adopt. Recognising this was very important – since it influenced the thinking about the key outcomes of the project. On the one hand strategy development was about developing systems, measures and reporting channels – process orientated activities that can happen relatively quickly, and on the other, it was about education, understanding and engagement – developing an embedded understanding of strategic priorities so that key leaders can direct, influence and lead. The latter element is essential to the development of a sustainable strategic capability (see Box 4.1).

Box 4.1 Some keys to success

1 Develop an embedded understanding (through education and engagement) of strategic priorities. This allows leaders to direct, influence and lead. The latter is essential to the development of a sustainable strategic capability.
2 Cascade an effective framework and make it meaningful. The University's ability to transfer skills from within a central project team into the wider organisation is essential.
3 Use a variety of communication approaches to engage members of staff at all levels and encourage them to think about how they make a difference in their role.
4 Ensure information to support strategic review is in a form that is useful, accurate and easily digestible, and that it helps to reinforce focus.

Translate the strategy to operational terms

This principle is about ensuring that the strategy is defined clearly so that it can be managed and implemented. The University developed a single University 'strategy map' to provide a clear, simple, summarised representation of the University's strategy – illustrating the key objectives (grouped into themes) to achieve the overall University vision (see Figure 4.2).

The objectives and themes within the map were been positioned to represent the priorities for the University of Leeds, hence, unlike many private sector 'strategy maps', finance is a key enabler rather than an overriding objective.

In order for the map to be recognisable to our staff, students and stakeholders, the language used had to be changed to reflect our purpose (for example – the terms 'stakeholders' and 'partners' more accurately reflect our key external relationships than would the term 'customers'). The map provided an extremely useful vehicle for focusing debates, providing a common reference point for all staff across the organisation to plan priorities. Whilst relatively simple, the map is very busy compared to those of a number of other organisations and over time it will most probably become simpler with fewer priorities. The positioning of the objectives on the map was important as they demonstrate a cause–effect relationship, flowing from the strategic enablers through the main strategic themes on the map into the objectives at the top of the map representing the value our stakeholders and partners seek from the University. The development of the map took two or three iterations to move from the initial version produced by the strategy group to the final launch version.

The process of creating a map that struck the right balance between complexity and simplicity whilst being able to be meaningful, recognisable and valuable was very difficult to achieve. Trying to represent the objectives and aspirations of a very broad and large institution on a single side of A4 really forced the strategy group to consider priorities. The 'strategy map' was supported by a series of 'definitions' for each objective on the map – enabling a more detailed understanding of the meaning and rationale for each objective.

The second part of translating the strategy into operational terms concerned developing a 'balanced scorecard' to define and measure key strategic outputs. The starting point for the development of this 'scorecard' was the 'strategy map' – taking each of the 31 objectives on the 'strategy map' and developing 'measures' which could be used to provide a high level indication of performance against strategic targets. This process was very difficult, because the 'strategy map' was developed with a very clear focus upon the objectives to achieve the University's long-term vision and was not influenced by considerations about ease of measurement. The development of measures was undertaken with a view to being able to provide a simple indication of the level of performance against strategic targets using a traffic light system of

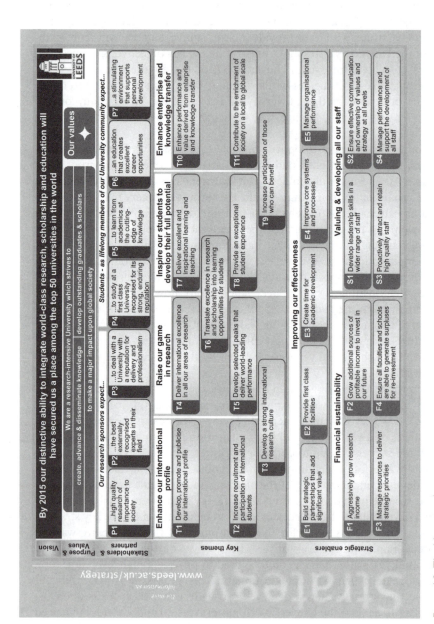

Figure 4.2 The University's strategy map.

Source: The University of Leeds: www.leeds.ac.uk/strategy

red, amber and green indicators. For most objectives on the map, a number of indicators were defined, providing both 'leading' and 'lag' indications of performance. For example – when looking at the objective to 'provide an exceptional student experience' – the lag or outcome measure identified was based around the results of our student survey, whereas the lead measure looked at student–staff ratio, a key underpinning element of an exceptional student experience. This development work resulted in an initial framework of over 60 independent measures. For each of these measures to be meaningful, targets had to be set to provide a benchmark of strategic performance, and for most of the measures supporting targets had to be set for each faculty.

To provide focus and to enable the key priorities to be clearly understood and more easily communicated, the strategy group prioritised a subset of this total measure framework into a set of ten 'gold key strategic measures' supported by a 'scorecard' of around 30 measures. This prioritisation was important in order to avoid the momentum of the project stalling over a complex design activity (creating targets for 60 measures) that would take considerable time to complete and may cause members of staff to disengage from the process due to the level of complexity. The target setting approach chosen, around a focused set of measures, enabled the strategy process to be cascaded rapidly.

The first principle – *leadership* – was a very significant part of the development of the scorecard. Strong leadership around the key themes on the map was needed to put a structure and strategic context to the plethora of potential measures. It would have been very easy for the University to have lost its way within a 'measure soup' – a mixture of lead/lag, strategic/operational, short-term/long-term indicators all sitting together as an ill-defined mass of information. The leadership role was critical in agreeing a focused set of measures and using these then to support strategy reviews.

The third part of translating the strategy was concerned with defining immediate strategic priorities and developing University-wide 'initiatives' to focus development upon major strategic priorities. Work streams were created at both University and faculty level to address performance gaps aligned to the strategic priorities. Each University level initiative has a strategic sponsor responsible for their development and successful implementation – emphasising the importance of leadership and accountability.

Align the organisation to the strategy

The design of the cascade process is an important consideration in any strategy project. For the University of Leeds this presented a considerable challenge, with over 6,000 staff based in nine faculties and ten services. The cascade design considered how measures, objectives and initiatives in the University's strategy would be implemented throughout the University and how this cascade would be phased and supported. Careful thought was given to the cascade process, ensuring that there was clarity about the objectives of the initial cascade. It was important that this was seen as more than a 'planning process'. The initial cascade was facilitated by the central project team with the aim of developing teams' understanding and engagement as much as generating operational plans. The initial focus and priorities were around major academic units (faculties) and cross-cutting themes. An immediate priority after launching the University map was to cascade this into faculties and support them in identifying their own priorities to improve their future performance. This resulted in the development of a number of faculty-level initiatives to address performance gaps.

A second stage of the cascade involved faculties and schools developing local-level targets as part of their annual planning process that corresponded with University-level gold targets. Faculties will review performance against their targets at assigned strategy review meetings across the year. The linking of strategy with operational planning is key to the successful implementation of the strategy; faculty annual plans now include initiatives and targets to create focus and reinforce local engagement with the strategy.

Motivate to make strategy everyone's job

A number of different ways of communicating the strategy were developed, aiming to achieve very high levels of awareness and engagement. The communication campaign had a number of different layers and objectives. Building a strong understanding of the strategy, its underlying principles and priorities within the strategy amongst the key leaders across the University was a key early priority. This was never going to be effective if run as top-down communication, since the University need these leaders both to understand fully the strategy and have a sense of ownership of its development and execution. Hence the importance of getting very early active involvement during the development phase. To facilitate this interaction, the Vice-Chancellor introduced a leadership forum; a monthly meeting of senior leaders across the institution which provided an opportunity for strategic conversations and informal networking. Due to the success of this forum, a Heads of Service forum was also created, to improve communication and collaboration between Heads of Service. It soon became evident, however, that other complementary approaches were required to reach members of staff at different levels more directly. A number of open meetings were therefore held where members of staff were able to ask questions and hear first hand the Vice-Chancellor describe the challenges facing the University and how everyone has an important part to play. Other activities have included a question-and-answer live webcast with the Vice-Chancellor and members of staff and the making of a film demonstrating how everyone across the institution can make a strategic contribution. A key learning point for the University of Leeds is the need to use a variety of very different communication approaches to engage members of staff at all levels and encourage them to think about how they make a difference in their role.

Govern to make strategy a continual process

For any strategy to be effective there needs to be a mechanism for the objectives within the strategy to be governed. The governance approach needs to ensure that the organisation's performance is improving in line with the expectations set out within the strategy and also that supporting initiatives are appropriate and are sufficiently challenging the status quo. The balanced score card approach suggests that a critical success factor for strategy implementation is regular review; where strategic performance is constructively discussed at a senior level. The University's strategy group is responsible for the overall governance of the strategy and will therefore carry out regular strategic review meetings. At these meetings, the University's performance against its strategic intent will be debated and discussed. This is a significant challenge as it requires the production of supporting reports identifying changes in performance against strategic gold measures and regular progress reports from University-wide initiatives. The University of Leeds invested in performance management software to provide data on strategy performance. There is a temptation to overwhelm senior colleagues with performance data and operational detail; this, however, does provide them with space to debate the strategic priorities effectively. A key learning point is the need to ensure that information to support strategic review is in a form which is useful, accurate and easily digestible and which helps to reinforce focus. As the strategy cascade progresses it is anticipated that strategy review meetings will be held in faculties and schools on a regular basis creating local governance and these will provide input and regular progress reports for the University's strategic review.

Lessons learned and ongoing challenges

In summary, the chapter illustrates the importance of developing a strategy execution capability. Most corporate strategies are valid but very rarely fully implemented. The approach developed at the University of Leeds responds to this challenge, balancing the importance of the content of strategy and the capability to execute it. There are however a number of key learning points.

- The strategy process must have *top leadership sponsorship*, fully engaged in defining the long-term change agenda articulated through a compelling vision and strategy.
- Organisation level initiatives require a strategic sponsor responsible for their development and successful implementation – emphasising the *importance of dispersed leadership and accountability*.

- The initial stage of the project involves *building a strong consensus* amongst the senior managers for the case for change. A more open style of communication provides managers from all departments with the opportunity to have a voice in the strategy. This is an essential early foundation in developing commitment around the new vision.
- *Time* is needed *to translate strategy into operational terms* which provide focus. These are then cascaded to all members of staff to support engagement and ownership. This can be difficult to achieve in practice, as there is an inevitable tendency for leaders and managers to concentrate their time on day-to-day activities and business as usual rather than engaging with the complexity of the 'strategy' map process.
- Strategy delivery can be effectively supported by the development of a *'balanced scorecard' framework to manage performance*. There can be a tendency for the 'performance measurement' aspects to dominate the strategic agenda and this must be balanced as the culture of the organisation may not respond to a strategic framework being predominately measures-driven.
- For an organisation such as a university, feedback from a number of staff has indicated that *the balanced scorecard approach felt a little 'top-down' and commercially driven*. The language used in the strategy map was felt to be too direct and has been moderated to bring members of staff on board using language with which they were more familiar – e.g. substituting the word 'customers' for 'stakeholders' and 'partners' to describe the University's relationship with students and research sponsors.
- The balance scorecard framework approach alone did not create an opportunity to sufficiently consider the *University's values and the necessary environment needed to underpin successful strategy delivery*. UofL has added the organisational values on to the strategy map and is working to create the optimum environment for strategy delivery.
- *Strategic alignment* is a key part of the implementation challenge. For the strategy to be effectively cascaded throughout the University all traditional planning activities must be fully integrated and supportive of the strategic priorities.
- To make strategy everyone's job, a wide range of creative *communication approaches* are needed to create a sense of momentum and encourage engagement. The strategic messages need to be simple and continual to ensure that they filter through to all levels. The approach chosen should also encourage ongoing two-way feedback.
- Strategy must be fully *integrated into the governance* of the University, establishing strategy reviews and reporting processes to ensure ongoing focus upon the strategy.

It is anticipated that the University of Leeds will take a further three to five years to fully embed the strategic management framework and ensure that all members of staff appreciate how they can contribute to strategy and that this will be demonstrated in time through improved performance.

References

Bridges, W. (2005) *Managing Transtitions* (2nd edn), Nicholas Brearley Publishing: London.

Kaplan, R. and Norton, D. (2001) *The Strategy Focused Organisation*, HBS Press: Boston.

Kaplan, R. and Norton, D. (2004) *Strategy Maps*, Harvard Business School Press: Boston.

Niven, P. (2003) *Balanced Scorecard for Government and Nonprofit Agencies*, John Wiley and Sons: New Jersey.

Chapter 5

Change at the top

An evaluation of major changes to leadership, management and organisational structures at Anglia Ruskin University

Helen Valentine and Julian Constable

This chapter reports on management perceptions of the handling of a major change to organisational structures at Anglia Ruskin University. It indicates the background and context, outlines the rationale for the restructuring, discusses the views of those involved and concludes with the 'lessons learned' from the process.

The University context

Anglia Ruskin is a large and complex 'post-'92' UK university. It is based on two main sites, at Cambridge and Chelmsford, separated by 45 miles and with a large 'regional university partnership' comprising mainly of FE partners. Prior to the restructuring the organisation comprised many small central units and eight academic schools. It had also developed a highly flexible modular curriculum and had allowed proliferation of modules, pathways, modes and locations with the result that programme delivery was highly complex and resource inefficient. The lead researcher for this project arrived at Anglia Ruskin University as Pro-Vice-Chancellor in Autumn 2002 and led a number of streamlining and simplification initiatives during 2002–3 and 2003–4 in the areas of organisational and curriculum structures. The University also introduced a wide-ranging set of revisions to HR policies and procedures, concentrating on changes to the role of academic staff and including a significant voluntary severance scheme.

A QAA institutional audit held in May 2004 delivered a judgement of 'limited' rather than 'full' confidence in Anglia Ruskin University. This was a serious blow to the staff in the University. The central concerns of the review team were not about the underlying quality of teaching and learning but about the complexity of roles and inconsistent application of the QA processes. They were complimentary about the staff support and development systems and the learning and teaching infrastructure.

The complexity of structures, processes and their consequences resulted in a system that the Vice-Chancellor described on his arrival as 'entirely unmanageable'. This view reinforced and gave impetus to debates and actions concerning structural and other key changes that had already started.

The summer of 2004 also coincided with the arrival of a new Vice-Chancellor who initiated a revised mission for the University and set in train a process of consultation on a new strategic plan. The new VC has since led the implementation of widespread and far-reaching changes to almost every aspect of the strategies and structures of the University. These changes were necessary in any event, but the QAA audit outcome gave them an obvious urgency and priority. There had been few major changes in the University for a number of years, at a time when the external environment had been changing rapidly. The University was an environment that Weick and Quinn (1999) would describe as needing 'episodic' rather than incremental change.

This convergence of what Trowler *et al.* (2003) have called 'chronic features' (i.e. pre-existing problems such as the complex and inefficient structures) and the 'conjunctional features' (i.e. the new imperatives such as the QAA verdict and a new VC) served to combine and create an immediate and powerful impetus for change and to reduce the resistance to it.

The common theme pervading all of the changes was the aim to simplify structures and processes and clarify accountabilities. It was felt that sorting out these underlying problems would, in due course, allow the University to concentrate more of its energy on its core academic activity. This was and is necessary for building the reputation of the University, as well as for ensuring economic viability. This model of change does assume that changes to structures and process are causally and sequentially linked to improved organisational performance, as described by Porras and Silvers (1991).

The organisational restructuring project, which is the subject of this report, is a key building block in this overall transformation of the University. It is made particularly challenging and interesting because it was one of a package of parallel initiatives which, taken together, will change almost every aspect of the University over a period of two to three years.

Planning the changes to the organisational structure

The structural change involved the transformation of eight schools and 24 central units into a structure comprising five faculties and 12 central units over a short and intense period of about six months.

The objectives of this change for Anglia Ruskin University were numerous but included:

* the need to simplify and streamline complex and inefficient structures to clarify responsibilities and reinforce accountabilities (internal and external analysis suggested this was lacking);

- the need to build academic critical mass and maximise synergies between academic disciplines within large cross-University faculties (small single-campus schools made this difficult);
- the need to align internal faculty structures with 'regional faculty' structures set up to manage the complex regional partnerships. The University had some 25 mainly FE partners at the time the restructuring process began. These relationships were also being simplified through a related change project;
- the desire to ensure that all academic activity was located within one of the five faculties. Previously some of the central units ran taught short courses and delivered research and/or consultancy projects;
- the desire to have one executive decision-making group involving Directorate, Heads and Deans working together. This group was to be called the (SMG Senior Management Group). Previously Deans, but not Heads, were included in the senior decision-making group. There had also been a wider group (the Management Operations Group (MOG)) comprising almost 40 managers which was widely believed to be ineffective as a decision-making forum (see Figures 5.1 and 5.2).

These changes were debated by Directorate, the Corporate Management Group (CMG), Management Operations Group (MOG) and to some extent within faculties and services before being finalised. All staff were invited to submit comments to the Vice-Chancellor. The adequacy of this consultation process is reported as part of the results.

The evaluation process

Scope of the restructuring

Some of the key human aspects of this organisational change were:

- a revised view concerning the expectations of senior managers at Anglia Ruskin University. A document was written by the PVC which outlined the qualities desired in the 'ideal' senior manager. This paper was debated by senior managers before being finalised. This paper formed a backdrop to the recruitment process. It articulated expected skills, behaviours and values for those who took jobs in the new structure;
- a period of uncertainty and intense pressure for senior staff, who were concerned about their future role and status within the organisation. Once appointed they were then immediately asked to settle into their own new roles at the same time as managing a range of other changes, including supporting colleagues in new roles within the faculties and central services;
- the practicalities and the perspectives of managers involved in the

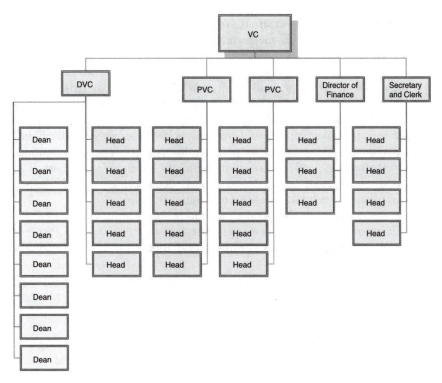

Figure 5.1 Management structure: before the restructuring.

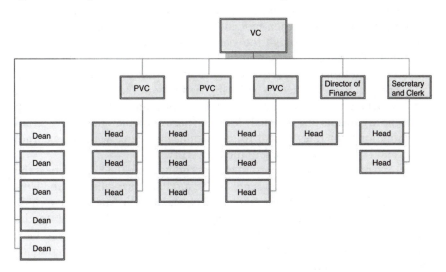

Figure 5.2 Management structure: after the restructuring.

selection and appointment processes as interviewees and interviewers. The University used external consultants to conduct an 'assessment centre' involving psychometric tests and role play exercises, followed by formal panel interviews. All internal as well as external candidates were asked to undertake these tests;

- the additional HR workload involved in agreeing new pay structures for the new roles, arranging the numerous interviews and dealing with a range of disappointed and displaced staff;
- the need to deal sensitively and creatively with the senior staff 'displaced' from their previous roles as part of this process. The restructuring, together with a need to manage retirements on a more active basis, has led to the agreed, planned and phased departure of over 20 senior managers between Summer 2004 and Summer 2006;
- the desire to ensure that strides made in terms of improving the gender balance of the University senior management were not lost in the process of restructuring, whilst also ensuring that appointments were made on the basis of merit;
- the individual and team staff development needs arising from this change across the senior management team as a whole and within each new faculty and new central unit.

Most of the data collection for this project occurred during the spring and early summer of 2005. This was around nine months since the major restructuring changes were first debated and around three to six months from implementation. The timing of this 'snapshop' almost certainly had an important bearing on the results. Bridges (1986) describes three stages of psychological transition when individuals are faced with a change: 'ending and letting go'; going through the 'neutral zone' and finally 'making a new beginning'. The results suggest that some managers were still dealing with the early-stage emotional aspects of the change at the time of the research.

This project was confined to gathering views about the processes involved in the restructuring itself. The chapter does not attempt to analyse in any depth the arguments and rationale for or against particular alternative structural solutions nor does it deal to any significant degree with the external context and market positioning of the University.

There were many other important changes going on in the University at the same time including: major revisions to the modular curriculum in the University; to the University name (the name changed from Anglia Polytechnic University to Anglia Ruskin University in September 2005) and to the regional partnership arrangements. Many of the respondents appear to have been unable or unwilling to disaggregate these changes when responding to the survey. The impact of the structural change itself cannot therefore be viewed in isolation from the other parallel change projects.

The data collection

The survey which informs this chapter was designed to achieve an understanding of the views of senior managers concerning the processes of organisational change 'before', 'during' and 'after' the restructuring. Data was collected via means of a questionnaire and interviews. The overall response rate was 64 per cent.

The population for this survey consisted of 50 senior staff at Anglia Ruskin University who had been members of a previous management group called the Management Operations Group (MOG), plus faculty Associate Deans. About half of this population were members of the new group formed after restructuring – the Senior Management Group (SMG).

The survey was followed by seven semi-structured interviews which lasted between 45 and 75 minutes each. These were conducted on a non-attributable basis by the project assistant.

Summary results and discussion

The overall response rate was good and the questionnaire and interviews together provided a 'rich picture' of the views of managers. The written comments in response to each question in the survey were particularly illuminating.

The Directorate were the group most supportive of the changes. Deans and Heads were generally more negative overall than other groups in the survey. The Directorate support and engagement is unsurprising since they initiated and led the restructuring process. The concerns held by some Deans and Heads is more worrying. It does have to be borne in mind that in small samples such as these one or two very negative respondents can have a big influence on the results. The comments suggested that it was Deans rather

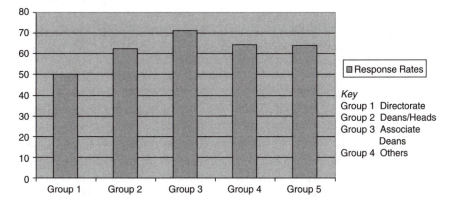

Figure 5.3 Senior staff survey response rate.

than Heads who had the strongest reservations with some aspects of the process and outcomes:

> I sense a reluctance on behalf of the Directorate to work cooperatively and collaboratively with the Deans.

> The dislocation between the Directorate and the faculties, the failure to involve key stakeholders and the continuation of ineffective committees are major problems.

Almost 80 per cent of Associate Deans were new internal appointments. They were positive about many aspects of the changes. The 'others' in group 4 were generally very positive given that most of these had not benefited from the changes. Some of these staff had been 'displaced' through the restructuring whilst some had ceased to be members of the Senior Management Group forum.

A very interesting finding was that there appeared to be quite a large degree of difference between the average response to questions about structures, strategies, objectives and outcomes (what might be described as 'hard' or 'what' factors) where, in general, there was widespread agreement and mostly positive responses:

> There is no doubt that we are headed in the right direction.

> I fully agree with the VC's assessment: the old organisational structure was inappropriate and incapable of delivering the business objectives.

> I have not heard a dissenting voice at senior level.

This contrasts with the results for questions more concerned with processes, consultations, feeling and emotions (i.e. what might be described as 'soft' or 'how' factors) where, in general, there was a more negative response:

> They [Deans and Heads] are under enormous pressure. My personal view is that workloads are unreasonable at this point but I hope they will settle down.

The recurring themes from the comments were that the restructuring had been a painful but necessary process. There was widespread agreement that change was necessary and urgent and even that these particular changes were the right ones. The concern was mainly about how this change has impacted at a practical and emotional level on staff, particularly for middle managers. The new structure, coupled with new expectations, has resulted in key managers being much more visible and accountable than before. Respondents also felt that the Directorate style has changed and most, but not all, thought that this was a negative development. There are important issues of trust and autonomy which are still being resolved:

> Decision-making seems very focused on the VC/Directorate. This does not empower senior managers.

A summary of the main concerns arising from the questionnaire results include the following:

- The perceived *inadequacy of the consultation processes* and *timescales* leading up to the restructuring. This might also be described as a failure to delineate clearly between consultation and communication, i.e. what was and was not 'up for grabs'. 'Although there was some consultation I am not sure that the responses were always heard.'
- Some remaining concerns about the *new faculty and service boundaries* and whether these are entirely satisfactory. This implies that the University needs to keep the new structure under review and that some further changes might be required.
- Some feeling that the *overall vision of the University* is still *not clear* and/ or is insufficiently focused on academic issues. There is also a strong consensus that in the first year there was too much concentration on short term operational plans and budgets and not enough on longer term strategic issues. It is felt that this will become problematic if the emphasis does not change soon.
- Criticism of *communication processes*, including a feeling that some staff are 'too distant' from the decisions, that the Directorate is too powerful and doesn't seek to involve the Deans and that information needs are not always being met. 'A whole layer of communication structures has been removed so I and others feel very distanced from decision-making processes.'
- A feeling that the *revised senate committee structure* is better than before but still not perfect and is still *too cumbersome*. Deans feel that Senate has concentrated too much on exposing faculty weaknesses in sometimes unhelpful ways.
- Some *disappointment with the operation of the new Senior Management Group* (SMG) and a feeling that it is still 'bedding down'.
  'It [SMG] permits greater transparency because it is smaller but it has not yet developed its full potential.'
- Heads and Deans feel that SMG will work better only when *trust* has been built sufficiently to *make it 'safe'* to criticise Directorate proposals.
- A continuing worry about *communication with* and about the *regional FE partners* and the adverse effect this apparent lack of clarity has on decision-making for Deans and Heads.
- Some concern about whether there is the *capacity and capability* within

the senior team as a whole (including within the Directorate) *to achieve the challenges that the University has set itself.* 'I worry about this. We have taken on a demanding set of objectives. Not all senior managers are sufficiently motivated or skilled to do everything we require of them.'

- There is also concern about the *undervaluing of past achievements* and of the failure to acknowledge the different cultures and histories of the two campus traditions. Nadler-Tushman (1980) emphasise the importance of factors such as understanding history and informal organisational arrangements in ensuring success with new structures.

- A feeling from some, particularly Deans and Heads, that the *Directorate does not fully understand the day to day work in the faculties and central services* and sometimes makes ill-informed decisions as a consequence.

- A very significant worry about *workload, stress and morale issues* for managers and senior academic staff. Beer and Baghat (1985) developed a model of understanding stress in relation to the uncertainty of outcomes, importance of those outcomes and duration of the uncertainty. All of these have been factors for senior staff.

- A feeling that individuals are expected to carry responsibility for issues where there has been a *failure of data and or systems* and that improving these should be a priority for the University.

The interviews provided some useful additional data and context. They reinforced the view that there was a very wide range of perception of the changes overall, from strong support and a dismissive attitude to those opposing the change, through to deeply held reservations about much of the process. 'Some people will always be unwilling to change . . . and will find any rationale they can to dress this up in some semi-respectable clothes.'

These differences in views could be explained to some extent by differences in employment background, with more recent employees and those with a wider range of experiences external to the University perhaps less negative than longer-serving staff. 'Background impacts massively. My management/ leadership stance comes from one of being used to a contracting world. Gain contract, gain staff, lose contract, lose staff.'

There was some evidence that the differing campus cultures between Cambridge and Chelmsford were also influencing perceptions. The issues concerning staff workload and morale, the pace and scale of change and the relationship between Deans and Directorate were reinforced in the comments from the interviews.

Conclusions and recommendations

Lessons learned for Anglia Ruskin University

The University has learned much from this process and this will inform the handling of future changes.

The key points include the following:

- *The Vice-Chancellor and the Directorate must articulate the strategy, direction and need for change repeatedly.* It should not assume that this is universally understood or accepted or that other senior managers can do this on behalf of the Directorate.
- Directorate must not underestimate the *time-consuming nature of major change* and must produce a *detailed written project plan, an additional dedicated senior staff resource* and an explicit *communications strategy*.
- It is important to maintain a clear direction, not to be deflected from the overall objectives but to be prepared to respond to feedback and criticism and be flexible about the means of getting to the objective.
- The change process is not finished when the structural changes have happened. The process of cultural change has only just started at that point and more work still needs to be done.
- The use of 'displaced' senior staff in project roles has worked well. These staff have been and will continue to be a very useful resource to help embed the changes at a time when line managers have been fully stretched.

Lessons for other HEIs

It is not possible to be sure how much of this change is transferable to other circumstances but it appears to have followed much of the pattern predicted by the theory. This would suggest that it is safe to assume that some of the lessons may well be useful for other organisations undergoing similar structural change:

- Understand that it is possible (if not necessarily desirable) to achieve enormous change in a short time. The new structures and senior staff were in place six months from being debated and significantly improved organisational results were being achieved within a further six months.
- There is value in providing skilled and supportive external facilitation for team-building events with and between the new teams.
- It is useful to be clear and honest about what is and what is not up for consultation and to be prepared to be flexible in response to consultation feedback.
- Be aware of the enormous personal stress for those whose jobs are

affected by the restructuring. These staff cannot effectively communicate the University vision until their personal circumstances are resolved and their level of uncertainty reduced.

- Be considerate and fair to those staff 'displaced' by the process of change. These staff can act as a very considerable and important 'resource' to help cope with the extra work generated by the change process.
- *Hold ones nerve!* Heifetz (1994) described this process as 'holding the collective feet to the fire'. It is necessary for the VC to demonstrate this resolve, even when others all around are expressing concern.

Early assessment of the restructuring on the performance of the University

Eighty-four per cent of respondents agreed or strongly agreed with the statement 'I believe that the University is better placed to meet the challenges of the next ten years than before the restructuring process began.'

Of course the restructuring process itself was run in parallel with many other internal changes as well as changes in the external environment and it is very difficult to isolate cause and effect. Nevertheless there have been a number of positive signs during the past 6–12 months which provide grounds for optimism in terms of the overall indicators of University success. These include: improved trends in student recruitment, improved league table position, positive outcomes from all recent external quality audits, improved financial performance, large grants from two major funding bodies and a significant increase in external income generation. The name change has also had a very significant effect on morale and confidence in the organisation.

Overview of the evaluation project

The Leadership Foundation Fellowship project funding allowed and facilitated a more structured, thorough and independent evaluation than would otherwise have been possible. The restructuring was a major change for the University and the outcomes are of fundamental concern for the future health and prosperity of the organisation. The feelings, motivations and morale of senior managers are extremely important in determining the longer term success of the University and a thorough understanding of their views and concerns are therefore essential.

Much of the response highlighted aspects that have caused dissatisfaction and could have been done better. However there was near-universal agreement of the need for the University to change and widespread agreement with the nature of the changes made. The Directorate has endeavoured to learn from the criticisms surrounding the process of communication and consultation and has taken actions to address the key issues.

References

Beer, T. A. and Bhagat, R. S. (1985) *Human Stress and Cognition in Organisations: An Integrated Perspective*, John Wiley and Sons: New York.

Bridges, W. (1986) 'Managing organisational transitions', *Organisational Dynamics*, 15(1): 24–33.

Heifetz, R. A. (1994) *Leadership Without Any Easy Answers*, Harvard University Press: Cambridge, MA.

Nadler, D. A. and Tushman, M. L. (1980) 'A model for diagnosing organisational behaviour', *Organisational Dynamics*, Autumn: 35–51.

Porras, J. I. and Silvers, R. C. (1991) 'Organisation development and transformation', *Annual Review of Psychology*, 42: 51–78.

Trowler, P., Saunders, M. and Knight, P. (2003) *Change Thinking, Change Practices: A Guide to Change for Heads of Departments, Programme Leaders and Other Change Agents in Higher Education*, Learning and Teaching Support Network, Generic Centre: York.

Weick, K. E. and Quinn, R. E. (1999) 'Organisational change and development', *Annual Review of Psychology*, 50, 361–86.

Chapter 6

Developing leaders

A structured approach to the enhancement of organisational and individual performance

Malcolm Rhodes

The institutional context: organisational change and development

Recently established as the University of Chester, the former Chester College (and at one stage, prior to 1998, University College Chester) was established in 1839 as a Diocesan Teachers' Training College. Until the recent attainment of taught degree awarding powers and University status, it had, since 1920, awarded degrees of the University of Liverpool. For many decades during the nineteenth and twentieth centuries, the College, as an institution dedicated to teacher education, was able to function successfully with its leadership operating within a relatively static higher education sector and a stable funding environment. The dominant characteristic of institutional leadership throughout this long history has been stewardship, informed by a strong commitment to the Christian ethos of the institution and guided by reference to its Foundation.

In the rapidly changing and increasingly complex and competitive higher education environment which now prevails, the institution is required to strengthen its adaptive capacity. Further, through the development of effective leadership at all senior levels of the organisation, it must also ensure that the necessary process of continual renewal, with a constancy of purpose expressed through its distinctive Mission, assures its long-term future.

In the past decade, the organisation has experienced substantial growth in student numbers, with progressively accelerating and significant changes in its profile of activities and concomitant changes to its status. In 2003 the College was granted its own taught degree awarding powers with the consequent changes to its long-standing relationship with the University of Liverpool. The College achieved university status in August 2005.[1]

The pace and extent of these changes have made progressively greater demands on structures, processes and, particularly, people. Within this context the University is striving to maintain its organisational equilibrium and responsiveness and enhance its position in the region and in the higher education sector as a whole. The key to fulfilling these objectives is effective leadership and the continued successful management of change.

In 2004, in preparation for the implementation of its own taught degree awarding powers and in anticipation of university status, the institution's academic management structure was significantly revised. The new structure was designed to build the capacity to continue to grow as an organisation and to provide a more rational basis on which to manage and resource teaching, learning, research and curriculum change. This restructuring required the appointment of a significant number of senior postholders, either new to their roles or, in fewer cases, new to the institution. These postholders together with the Senior Management Team formed the University Executive. In this context, the devising and successful operation of a concerted, focused Leadership Development Programme to support these colleagues in their new roles became an increasingly important organisational priority.

Setting the direction

There is a substantial body of research on models of leadership and the impact of leadership styles on organisational effectiveness. It has emerged over several decades from numerous academic disciplines, ranging from business and management and organisational development, and human resource management, to the different perspectives offered by industrial and organisational psychology.

In setting the direction of the Leadership Development Programme within the University, a number of aims and objectives were agreed, focused on defining and promoting a clear understanding of the balanced relationship between organisational effectiveness and sustainability and the personal effectiveness and behaviours of the institution's leaders. The programme sought to prepare senior staff for leadership roles, not simply train them as institutional senior managers.

The concept of stewardship was adopted and consistently promoted by the Pro-Vice-Chancellor (Academic) leading the programme as the vehicle to reinforce the defining features of the University's approach to leadership development. This formed the enduring and guiding principle which under-pinned the philosophy, direction and activities of the programme.

As Peter Block suggests

> Stewardship . . . is to hold in trust the well-being of some larger entity – our organisation, our community. . . . To hold something of value in trust calls for placing service ahead of control. . . . There is pride in leadership, it evokes images of direction. There is humility in steward-ship, it evokes images of service.
>
> (1996: 41)

The approach

The approach to the Leadership Development Programme undertaken at Chester is most succinctly characterised as multidimensional, multiphased and multimethod.

Multidimensional

In determining the aims and direction of the Leadership Development Programme, many approaches were possible, on a continuum ranging from those which use corporate goals as the principal determinant of leadership skills and requirements, enabling leaders to develop competencies which are grounded in specific organisational and business goals and which are, by definition, largely context-specific, to those which are based on traditional development programmes, often abstract and generic, designed to meet the requirements of specific management qualifications frameworks, which often fail to meet corporate needs (London 2002). Reflecting the conclusions of the work of Longenecker and Neubert (2003), the University considered that a partnership approach between the organisation and the individual appeared to offer the greatest prospect of success.

It was evident that in order to generate sustainable performance improvement geared specifically to the needs of the organisation and simultaneously to reflect the career development priorities and aspirations of individual senior managers, it was necessary to adopt a multidimensional approach which recognised that leadership development is not merely a series of single events such as appraisal interviews or training courses, but, rather, comprises a long-term, continuing process of goal-setting, training and development activities, and performance analysis and review, progressively effecting changes in behaviour. This approach supported the view that the most effective leadership development programme transforms an event into a process that can endure throughout the participant's career (Zenger *et al.* 2000).

In this way, the programme sought to promote transformational, adaptive and principled leadership to reflect the University priorities in succession planning; to respond to the career aspirations of individual senior managers; and to establish a system to support the enhancement of individual performance.

This multidimensional approach was based on the view that efforts to 'teach' leadership skills often become 'disassociated from context and experience, undermining the education, most commonly by reducing it to analysis . . . [whereas] deep-rooted practical experience . . . turns the classroom into a rich arena for learning' (Gosling and Mintzberg 2004). In the commitment to maintain this balanced approach between the organisation and the individual, it was essential to locate in practice the theoretical and reflective learning within the Leadership Development Programme. The programme was therefore constructed to focus on collective learning and development designed to enhance organisational effectiveness and was concerned with producing shared values and consistency in style and approach across a range of organisational contexts. It was also concerned to promote individual, self-paced learning designed to improve individual ability and performance within the organisation (and the wider higher education sector).

The structure, form and content of the programme reflected the findings of recent research which supports the view that the most effective learning for managers occurs in the workplace (Longenecker and Neubert 2003). The programme was also developed and adapted to take account of the rapidly growing trend towards more personal forms of learning support: mentoring, coaching, 360° feedback, secondments and directed learning relevant to the working context.

Multiphased

The institution had instigated a Management Development Programme in 2002 for the cadre of senior managers and directors of service within the (then) College involving approximately 40 staff. The programme was designed to equip the College managers with the skills, awareness and exposure to good practice that would promote and sustain personal and organisational development and performance improvement.

The multiphased programme sought, in three segments operating over several years, to convey the sense of a developmental journey, both organisationally and individually.

In its initial phase, the programme focused on generic management development for the individual, exposing managers to general management principles relating to, for example, strategic management and organisational effectiveness. It was designed to promote the necessary skills and awareness and provide exposure to good practice that would enable them to contribute to organisational development and institutional performance improvement.

The second phase sought to promote the alignment of individuals in support of corporate strategic objectives. The vehicle for this second phase of development was the programme of (externally facilitated) Action Learning Sets.[2] This phase of the programme prepared the ground for the transition from management development based on generic organisational perspectives, to the manager and shifting the focus to the relationship between effective individual performance and organisational solutions.

However, it was in the third phase of the programme, responding to the specific needs to support the work of the newly established University Executive, that the Leadership Development Programme created the greatest impact at senior level within the University.

This phase of the programme sought to highlight the qualities and impact of effective leadership; to provide role models and to reaffirm appropriate leadership behaviours for the wider group of institutional managers; and to enable the institution to build the leadership capacity and styles to assure its own future in an increasingly complex and challenging environment.

Specifically, the aims of the programme were:

- to promote effective change management to enable the institution to fulfil its strategic aims to achieve University status and to professionalise its approach to management and organisational development; and
- in the context of the age and experience profile of the current Senior Management Team, to establish a framework for succession planning for leadership and management roles within the institution.

Multimethod

This third phase represented a shift in emphasis from managerial skills and competences to leadership attributes, creating an environment in which all managers were encouraged to challenge the status quo, to question conventional wisdom and existing practice, and to transform their own areas of work, consistent with the vision and strategy of the organisation. This required the needs of individual participants to be established: their roles, strengths, styles, attributes, dispositions and contributions to organisational effectiveness generating a personal development programme to improve individual and organisational performance.

Programme management

The Pro-Vice-Chancellor (Academic), having been awarded a Fellowship of the Leadership Foundation in 2005, was responsible for the management of the programme and initially sought advice on the structure of the programme from a senior colleague (recently appointed as the Head of the Department of Leadership and Management within the Business School of the University). The model of development finally adopted built on the multimethod approach that was being developed for use in leadership development programmes for a wide range of commercial and public sector clients.[3]

Programme structure and content

Prior to its launch, participants were invited to contribute to the structure and form of the programme to ensure that the agenda was self-designed to direct individual senior managers towards effective performance; to encourage the challenging of existing mindsets; to highlight personal accountability, collective responsibility and innovation; and to promote creativity and team work across Departments and Schools, crucial to the attainment of organisational objectives. This consultation period was essential to the success of the programme in affirming the participants' control of the programme and the significance of their role in the determination of its objectives.

The structure and content of the programme itself (see Figure 6.1) involved numerous development methods and techniques which provided the variety essential to retain participants' commitment and continuing engagement with the process. These included:

- personal development planning involving 360° feedback;
- coaching and mentoring by Senior Management Team members;
- external short courses;
- leadership development seminar programme;
- self-directed learning.

Personal development planning

A key stage in establishing the structure and content of the programme was the establishment of an agreed set of organisational values and priorities (see Figure 6.1). The construction of the personal development plan was based on a leadership gap analysis undertaken by participants within the context of that framework of values and organisational priorities[4] and an assessment the leadership skills required to deliver these objectives.

The process of self-assessment was facilitated on a confidential basis with individual participants working directly with an external consultant. This provided an important and reassuring sense of objectivity and 'distance' for the participants.

This work was supported by an extensive process of 360° feedback. In this process each participant was invited to nominate up to ten colleagues comprising the person to whom they reported, peers with whom they worked closely and members of the department which they led and managed. Each participant received detailed and lengthy confidential feedback from the consultant, during which process participants completed the Myers Briggs Type Indicator (MBTI), a well-established personality type preference feedback instrument. This process enabled the participants to construct a personal development plan to assist in the achievement of their (and the organisation's) objectives and in the identification of the support networks they would require.

The personal development planning process was designed to integrate individual participants' learning and development needs and preferences, areas of interest and organisational focus.

Coaching and mentoring

The University Executive had been established as part of a recent reorganisation of the University management structure and comprised the Senior

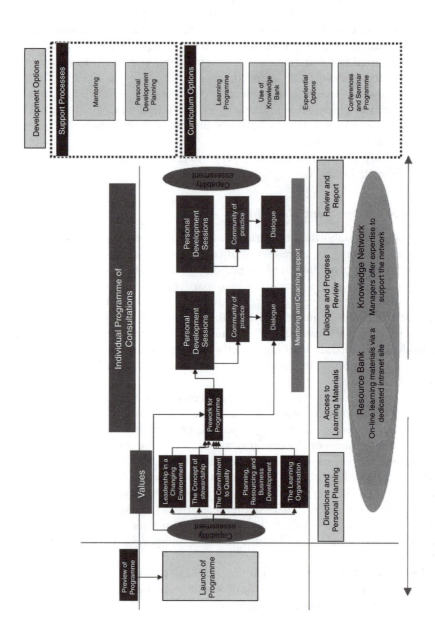

Figure 6.1 Leadership programme structure and content.

Management Team and ten Deans, seven with academic line management responsibility and three with University-wide roles. Many of the Deans were appointed at the time of the reorganisation and, whilst not new to the University (since many were formerly Heads of Department), the postholders were undertaking new roles and responsibilities. In this context, formal mentoring arrangements were established in which a member of the Senior Management Team acted as mentor to (normally) three of the ten appointees. Meetings were regular, formal and confidential. Mentor training was provided for the members of the Senior Management Team and the mentorship arrangements were organised in order specifically to avoid coinciding with the existing line management structures.

For the Senior Management Team it was agreed that external mentorship was appropriate and potentially most beneficial. This was arranged through an external contact of the Leadership Foundation Associate attached to advise the Pro-Vice-Chancellor (Academic) on the project. Key senior staff operating in cognate areas of responsibility in a range of institutions across the sector readily agreed to act as mentors to specified members of the Senior Management Team.

External short courses

As part of the programme, three members of the University Executive were invited to attend the Leadership Foundation 'Preparing for Senior Strategic Leadership' (see www.lfhe.ac.uk) programme early in 2006. The University considered that in view of the value which had clearly been derived from the Leadership Development Programme, additional exposure to broader strategic leadership issues was potentially beneficial. The participants within the University programme were selected through a process of written application, again, to ensure that the value and the level of University commitment to them was clearly demonstrated. The feedback from this programme was extremely positive.

Leadership development seminar programme

A generic leadership seminar programme was organised, commencing with the induction and assessment process and comprising lectures, open forums, mentor meetings, with significant external input from the public and private sectors. A range of senior staff from within and beyond the University sector gave presentations and engaged in reflection and analysis with the programme participants.

Self-directed learning

This aspect of the programme was the most innovative in that it provided the basis on which participants could engage with the substantial and rapidly growing literature on leadership and management. It was balanced by a customised approach to learning which recognised that interests and needs vary and that senior managers in higher education (indeed in many different public and private sector contexts) have limited time to engage with developmental learning materials.

The Pro-Vice-Chancellor (Academic), as Project Director, engaged the support of a senior member of staff in the University Department of Communication and Information Technology Services (CITS) to develop an intranet-based resource that could link to existing training and development materials and events from a range of different sources, including the Leadership Foundation. This was created as a dedicated site within the University intranet, password-protected and accessible only by the programme participants. The Pro-Vice-Chancellor (Academic) constructed an 'opinion piece' for each of the five core institutional values (see Figure 6.1). These set the organisational context and challenged the readers to assess the relevance and relationship of the agreed core values to the over-arching objectives of the newly-established University of Chester. Also, utilising the subject-based expertise of senior library staff and specialist staff from the Department of Leadership and Management, the opinion pieces directed programme participants to specialist e-resources which focused specifically on each of the core values.

This facility promoted the sharing of information and increased the depth of learning available to participants and was regarded as an extremely valuable resource supporting the programme. The intranet site enabled the participants to communicate confidentially, sharing thoughts, ideas and criticisms of the learning materials and, more generally, to reflect on the programme as a whole.

The site provided two key elements of support during the programme. The first element was a *resource bank* consisting of a set of on-line resources[5] providing access to substantial, but clearly navigated and focused e-resources from a range of leadership and management websites (including the Leadership Foundation) and to a large number of electronic journals. The selection of, and navigation through e-learning materials provided an accessible and manageable workload for the programme participants, geared directly to their learning needs and interests and the available time.

The second element consisted of an infrastructure to facilitate a 'knowledge network' through which managers could offer particular expertise to support and advise others within the programme. This web-enabled informal network proved to be invaluable to a group of staff who were relatively new to their roles. This method of sharing experience and expertise as well as more widely through face-to-face interaction, created a learning support group – essentially, a 'community of practice'. An informal meeting of the Deans outwith the University Executive Group was also effectively adapted to serve as a community of practice, moving to the consideration of actions, outputs and impact, with the emphasis on the development of sharing experience to tackle leadership issues.

This model of leadership development is being successfully utilised by the Department of Leadership and Management at the University of Chester in increasingly diverse contexts. It provides the basis for the design and delivery of leadership development for commercial and public sector clients, including large local authorities as they engage with the issues of the development of senior staff required to lead major organisational change. This approach has proved to be extremely successful since it provides a demonstrably effective combination of organisationally determined but individually focused personal and professional development.

Programme evaluation

The essence of the summary evaluation was to determine evidence of impact. The evaluation of the programme was conducted through a series of processes: a summative seminar involving the programme participants led by the Director of Programme Development from the Leadership Foundation; individualised questionnaire returns from the participants; and meetings organised by the Pro-Vice-Chancellor (Academic) with the individual participants. The project evaluation was made available to the wider sector through the channels of the Leadership Foundation at the major dissemination Conference in November 2005. Within the context of a generally successful programme, there were several aspects of its evaluation which should be highlighted.

First, the process of initial (and accurate) self-evaluation was essential. The initial self-evaluation and development needs analysis provided the participants with a measurable *base-line of performance* at the outset of the programme. The process of 360° feedback on performance and the formulation of personal development plans built on this base-line. This process ensured ownership of the participants' own programme of learning, reflecting their particular development needs and also confirmed the locus of control of the process of development.

Second, the approach to the *development of e-resources* was innovative. The construction of an agreed set of institutional core values and the creation of focused learning materials, connected to a wide range of external resources and knowledge banks, and clearly navigable through the intranet site was highly successful and is proving to be an effective approach in the provision of leadership and management development which the University is undertaking for commercial and other public sector bodies.

Third, the participants found particular value in the *leadership development seminars* which exposed them to a range of approaches and leadership styles of significant figures in higher education and other public sector organisations. The external input to the seminar programme was of an extremely high standard and punctuated the programme throughout the year with opportunities to reflect on the fundamentals of leadership in large organisations.

Fourth, from the viewpoint of the individual participants, a primary objective was to clarify their own *personal career development* ambitions and priorities. The programme was successful in that regard, although, interestingly, a number of participants determined not to plan further career advancement into more senior managerial roles. From their individual perspectives (and organisationally) this was a valuable outcome.

Predictably in such a wide-ranging programme, two aspects of the programme were less successful.

First, the *internal coaching and mentoring* arrangements were only partially successful and the benefit for participants was variable. This appeared to be attributable to different factors in specific contexts: the lack of experience of some mentors in this role (although formal staff development had been provided); the difficulty in a relatively small team of ensuring an objective 'distance' between mentor and mentored; and, in some cases, a reticence and a scepticism regarding the value of mentoring (natural in senior staff whose success is normally self-evident from their position and status). Nonetheless, it is clear from this experience that at senior level, that the difficulty of establishing mentorship arrangements external to the institution is far outweighed by the value of exposing colleagues to the experience, insight and guidance offered by senior managers in other institutions.

Second, the *extent of the management time* and input to the programme was significantly greater than originally anticipated. It was essential that the significance of the leadership development programme for senior staff was demonstrated by responsibility for the management and organisation of the programme resting with a member of the University Senior Management Team. However, in this case, the Pro-Vice-Chancellor (Academic) was also a participant. At times, this proved a difficult balance to maintain. Whilst demonstrable institutional support for such a programme is necessary, it is essential to ensure that a non-participant Project Director is appointed to manage and administer such programmes.

Overview

Within the context of a series of new appointments to senior roles and institutional issues relating to succession planning, the intention of the programme was to highlight the qualities of effective leadership, ensuring that the institution is able to build the leadership capacity and styles necessary to assure its own future in an increasingly complex and challenging environment.

This approach to leadership development has enabled the organisation to prepare for future challenges and to facilitate adaptation to a changing, more competitive environment. The decision at the outset to eschew the more traditional 'packaged' leadership development programmes in favour of this multidimensional, multiphased and multimethod approach, with participants' close engagement with external role models, has been vindicated.

This programme has provided a development model which has, in its most important aspects, been customised to each individual participant's learning needs. It has offered role models whose approach is characterised by high standards of moral and ethical conduct; inspirational motivation through the clear communication of a shared vision and high expectations; and participative leadership styles based on highly developed emotional intelligence. All of these are central to the successful delivery of the University Mission in the future.

Notes

1 An account of the development of the institution since its establishment in 1839 and the journey to university status is provided in *The University of Chester 1839–2005* by I. Dunn (2005) Chester Academic Press.
2 This technique encourages a team-based approach to practical problem-solving in the workplace. It is based on high performance, outcomes-directed learning which is of practical benefit to the participants and to the organisation (Teare *et al.* 2002).
3 Within the past two years this model has been progressively refined and is now successfully deployed in support of numerous substantial leadership development contracts which the University of Chester Business School has secured with major employers across the region through the work of the Department of Leadership and Management.
4 The Pro-Vice-Chancellor (Academic) secured participants' agreement on these values and priorities distilled from a range of documents, notably the organisational Mission Statement and the Corporate Plan. These statements were detailed and incorporated into the Leadership Foundation intranet site as part of the e-resources available to participants.
5 These resources were established by the Pro-Vice-Chancellor (Academic) in consultation with the Head of Department of Leadership and Management and senior learning resources staff.

References

Block, P. (1996) *Stewardship*, Berrett-Koehler: San Francisco.
Dunn, I. (2005) *The University of Chester 1839–2005*, Chester Academic Press: Chester.
Gosling, J. and Mintzberg, H. (2004) 'The education of practicing managers', *MIT Sloane Management Review*, 45(4): 19–22.
London, M. (2002) *Leadership Development*, Lawrence Erlbaum: New Jersey.
Longenecker, C. O. and Neubert, M. (2003) 'The management development needs of front-line managers: voices from the field', *Career Development International*, 8(4): 210–18.

Teare, R., Ingram, H., Prestoungrange, G. and Sandelands, E. (2002) 'High performance learning at work', *International Journal of Contemporary Hospitality Management*, 14(7): 375–81.
Zenger, J., Ulrich, D. and Smallwood, N. (2000) 'The new leadership development',
Training and Development, 54(3): 22–34.

Part 2

Incentivised approaches to leading and managing change

Chapter 7

Leading change in developing research and scholarship

The case of a teaching-intensive institution

Yahya Al-Nakeeb

Introduction

This chapter provides an overview of a Leadership Foundation for Higher Education (LFHE) Fellowship project that aimed at developing the research culture of a small teaching intensive College of Higher Education. The College is in a period of change and development and is currently pursuing degree-awarding powers and university title which requires providing evidence of advanced scholarship and professional competence. The chapter explores issues that may have a significant impact on this process and proposes strategies to overcome barriers such as the limited resources available to staff and the pressures on time allocated for research and scholarship.

The chapter offers no simple 'how to do it manual' as the issues faced were both complex and challenging. What is offered is an overview of the experience and strategies employed for leading change in research and scholarship in a small teaching-led institution.

Aims and objectives of the LFHE project

This project aimed to provide a model for the more coherent development of research and scholarship within what has been, traditionally, a teaching focused College of Higher Education. The work was underpinned by an institutional change programme designed to enable staff to support each other in engaging more systematically with sustainable scholarship and research.

The main objectives of the project were to:

- develop a framework for the integration of scholarship and applied research with teaching;
- encourage innovatory forms of curriculum development through the introduction of new forms of teaching and learning;
- develop a core group of staff who are research active in each department or across departments;

- support the research activity of staff who have a well established track record in research;
- encourage the creation of new research groups;
- explore possible collaborative scholarly activities, including joint publications, across departments.

At the heart of the approach lay a desire to transform the quality of both the staff and student experience. The change process is intended to produce outcomes that would do much more than merely generate curriculum-updating opportunities (although it is recognised that this is, in itself, an important activity). The approach to scholarship advocated added to the teaching role an additional dimension that saw the function of developing increasing critical awareness as a responsibility shared by students and staff alike. Such a synergy of expectations and demands assisted in the pioneering of dynamic new approaches to learning and teaching. The scope of the project also provided opportunities for personal and professional development by encouraging staff to share experiences and the outcomes of their work.

The setting

Newman is a Roman Catholic College of Higher Education which was founded in 1968 by the Catholic Education Service. Originally founded to train teachers for the Catholic schools in the Archdiocese of Birmingham and beyond, the College has grown from its original 300 to over 2,000 students. Around half of that growth has taken place over the past six years. The College continues to train teachers for both primary and secondary schools to provide continuing professional development and higher degrees for teachers and to work very closely with partnership schools in the Catholic sector as well as across the region.

The College has diversified into three schools of activity, Initial Teacher Training, Social Science and Humanities, and Community and Professional Development. It employs around 90 academic staff who take responsibility for the education of approximately 2,300 full-time and part-time students. The College has recently forged a strategic partnership with another relatively small HE College, Bishop Grosseteste, and a leading research institution, Leicester University, which validates its degrees.

Research and scholarship at Newman

As a teaching intensive HEI, Newman has not had a prominent research profile. The research conducted in the College is varied due to the diverse interests of subject staff. Research is conducted within and across subject areas, with some limited collaboration with other educational institutions. Increasingly, staff are expected to possess higher degrees and the College has moved towards a policy of attracting more staff with established research interest and publication history. Newman's main research focus is now on applied research which enables the development of appropriately targeted provision or which supports the College's engagement with the public and voluntary sector. In addition, the College has established mechanisms by which all staff are able to protect time for research and scholarly activity. This has been a challenge in an HEI which is, by nature of its provision, teaching intensive, but staff have welcomed the change and are actively seeking ways to take advantage of such opportunities. The establishment of a strong and vibrant Research Committee has proved a vital driver in the promotion of change.

Related literature

An increasing number of studies appear to show evidence of the benefits to students of being taught in departments with research active members of staff and the way this can improve their learning experience in the context of creating a culture of enquiry-based learning involving both staff and students (Boyer 1999, Brew 2001 and 2003, Durning and Jenkins 2005, Jenkins and Healey 2005). Research active staff, it is maintained, bring to the teaching commitments a level of intellectual renewal that adds to the quality of their work.

On the other hand, there has been relatively little research in this country on the way research and scholarship is developed in smaller teaching intensive higher education institutions. However, a number of studies have been carried out to explore the situation in small universities and polytechnics in Australia, Canada, New Zealand and the United States (Frank 2001, Furrow and Taylor 1996, Robertson and Bond 2005).

Planning

It is important to recognise the obstacles to developing a research culture at small universities, especially those that are perceived primarily as teaching institutions. These obstacles include: the absence of policies and systems that facilitate research, resistance from non-research oriented staff who feel threatened, the lack of graduate students to act as research assistants, above-average teaching and non-teaching commitments, the lack of time allocated for research and limited resources available for staff research and scholarly activity (Bazeley 1994, Frank 2001).

A number of issues and questions had to be considered and addressed, prior to drawing up an action plan. These questions included:

a) What does scholarship and research mean (e.g. basic, discovery or applied)?

b)   What is the problem (e.g. capacity, resources, volume or quality)?
c)   Why is the generation of research opportunities seen as important (e.g. identity, benefits to students)?
d)   What are the issues (e.g. culture, systems and structures)?
e)   What needs to be done (e.g. strategies, partnerships)?

Once the above issues were clarified, an action plan was agreed and a timetable was set for implementation (see Box 7.1).

Methodology

The current project centres on the work of six pilot groups of staff representing collaborative teams across departments and programmes within the College. These teams adapted an existing effective model of applied research and scholarship that has been developed in one of the College's departments. The project was led and coordinated by the LFHE Fellow who is also the College's Director of Research. His role involved providing intense support in the early stages of the project and guidance thereafter. Review meetings were held regularly in which participants were given the opportunity to share their overall perceptions of the processes and the predicted outcomes.

Having considered the level of experience of staff members and the absence of a critical mass of research in most departments, collaborative research (based on an existing successful model elsewhere in the College) was identified as the most appropriate approach. It was envisaged that experienced members of staff would work collaboratively with the less experienced staff on a piece of applied research. This type of research was also chosen in an attempt to guarantee a good rate of completion, for it was felt that staff would be driven by the desire to generate work that would enhance their teaching.

Staff were invited to express interest, in writing, in being involved in the

---

Box 7.1 Key milestones of the project

- Establishment of scholarship Forum
- Agreement of criteria for selection of pilot research groups
- Research groups selected and Action Plans produced
- Mid-point evaluation
- Generation of interim report and preliminary modelling of change management model
- Dissemination of initial findings to peers
- Full evaluation of implementation phase and writing of final report and planning of dissemination activities.

Fellowship Project. Criteria were set (see Box 7.2) for qualifying to be part of the pilot groups. Eleven written applications were received from departments, programmes, small groups and individuals. Following the evaluation of the bids by the Research Committee and consultation with the bidding groups, it was agreed that the Fellowship Project should be inclusive and try to accommodate as many of the research groups as possible. Therefore, a re-grouping of the 11 applications was envisaged as the most appropriate way forward. Six potential groups were identified and invited to participate in the project.

A workshop was organised for the groups to clarify issues regarding the process and to provide input on the writing up of the action plans. It was also agreed that the completed action plans should be submitted, along with a detailed research proposal and resource implications. The Research Committee provided a small grant for each group to kick start the project. A seminar was organised for all participants in which the action plan of each research group was presented by the lead person/s. The action plan included the topic, methodology, timescale, resources required and predicted outcome. Six projects with a total of 24 members of staff (27 per cent of all academic staff) were selected for the pilot groups. All projects focused on applied research with a strong pedagogical emphasis. The topics ranged from exploring the effectiveness of problem-based learning in psychology to enhancing literacy through the use of illustration and image. The groups included staff from across departments who shared mutual interests in research. It is important to note that staff were free to form their own collaborations. This significantly helped in terms of bringing together colleagues with similar interests, perspectives and ideas.

Box 7.2 Criteria for involvement in the project

1 Being able to provide evidence of existing staff interest in engaging more strategically with scholarly activity
2 Commitment to active purposeful engagement with the change programme
3 Being willing to produce, implement and disseminate an initial Scholarly Activity Action Plan based on the suggested development model
4 Agreement to contribute to the work of a Scholarship Project Forum that will regularly review and disseminate the work of the research group
5 Being able to identify the curriculum benefit linked to the planned scholarly development activities.

Support for research and scholarship

In order to develop its research culture, the College has initiated a number of policies and schemes aimed at supporting research and scholarship. The College articulated policies and processes to facilitate the conducting of research and to determine appropriate research projects, standards and ethics. The College produced guidelines on preparation of research proposals and the various support and funding schemes available to staff.

The College also provides specific enablers to support research and scholarship. These are the practical ways in which the institution supports research development, within the context of its shared attitudes, values, beliefs and norms. Two types of enablers were made available to staff: first, the 'hard enablers' which consisting of financial support, resources and time. Second, the 'soft enablers' which included support, encouragement, freedom of choice, project self-management and the building on strengths and 'know-how' (see Box 7.3). These were facilitated by the Fellow.

The 'hard enablers' provided by the College

Time allocated for scholarly activity

Members of staff are able to formally apply for a maximum of 30 days per year (term time) to pursue their scholarly activity. The allocated time is agreed between individual members of staff and their Head of Department or line manager, taking into account teaching and other commitments. The application should be based on previously identified needs through the annual staff appraisal process and has clear and measurable targets to be achieved.

Box 7.3 Incentives to engage staff with the research agenda

- 'Time' for scholarly activity
- Short sabbaticals
- Small grants
- Support with higher degree registration
- Support with conference costs
- Scholars' week
- Research seminars
- Workshops.

Negotiated short sabbatical

Two sabbaticals of half a term (maximum of six weeks) can be awarded to members of staff who are in their final stages of completing a higher degree (e.g. MPhil, EdD, PhD). The Head of Department or line manager approves the application and the department's staff support the nomination (if applicable). Expression of interest must be made at least two terms ahead of the planned time for the sabbatical.

Research committee small grants

These are awarded to support research, scholarship and creative achievement. Priority is given to collaborative research projects. These grants are made available to subject areas, research groups or individuals. A total of 12 awards are allocated annually to encourage members of staff to pursue small-scale research projects individually or as a group. This allocation is based on a competitive bidding process and an interim and final report is required as to the progress and outcomes of the project.

Support with higher degrees registration

The Research Committee normally provides up to 50 per cent of the registration fees for members of staff studying higher degrees in institutions other than Leicester University. Those who register with Leicester University are exempted from paying the registration fees.

Conference presentations

Research active staff are entitled to bid for financial support for presenting their own work at national or international conferences.

Scholars' Week

The reading week in the spring term is normally designated as Scholars' Week. Within this space staff are encouraged to work on their research projects.

Staff research seminars

These are monthly hosted seminars in which staff are encouraged to share both completed research and research-in-progress. The occasions constitute an opportunity for any interested staff to hear and debate the work of others. This strategy of shared seminars provides an example of an attempt to expose staff to the content knowledge and research processes of other departments. It was an attempt to weaken boundaries, thus contributing to 'shared values, beliefs, norms and attitudes' which can help to form a collective, rather than a purely departmental research culture.

Workshops

These are aimed at developing staff capacity to carry out research. They cover issues such as writing for publication, ethics in research and effective supervision of postgraduates.

Leading and managing the project

The style and type of leadership used in working with any group of people needs to be appropriate. The ability to instigate and manage change is an important quality for successful leadership of change management. Trust in and the integrity of the leader is paramount for success; they should be capable of providing inspiration, intellectual stimulation and individualised consideration. The leader must motivate colleagues to action by appealing to shared values and by satisfying the higher order needs of the group, such as their aspirations and expectations. This type of 'transformational leadership' provides vision and a sense of mission, instils pride and gains respect and trust. It also communicates high expectations and expresses important purposes in simple ways. An addition advantage is that it gives personal attention as the leader coaches and advises each person individually (Bass and Avolio 1994).

In leading the Fellowship project it was vitally important that the leader gave personal consideration, provided on-going and available support, continuous monitoring and knowledge inputs when needed. The leader had to 'drive out apprehension' in participants by supporting them in clarifying the research task and what was needed to produce a successful outcome. That apprehension had to be managed at the beginning of the project. Once that was achieved, involvement in scholarship and research was no longer perceived as threatening, on the contrary, it was seen as an added strength. Keys to overcoming apprehensiveness were the use of collaborative research projects and on-going and available support.

The Fellow worked with each group independently to provide help and/or advice when needed. This ranged from advice on the suitability of the College's software in handling a certain project's data to possible venues for the dissemination of results. The rate of progress of each of the six pilot groups was variable. But none of them gave cause for concern. The monitoring at the early stages was intensive but gradually required a lighter touch as individual and collective confidence and group cohesion grew.

Results and findings

The emerging evidence from the project indicates that small institutions can overcome some of the many challenges and demands on time to pursue a programme of viable research. Indeed, work of this type brings with it some advantages, such as more opportunities for dialogue and collaboration amongst staff on a small campus. Working collaboratively can be a way to overcome some of the limitations of time and resources. However, careful planning is needed to develop a critical mass of staff who have common research interests and who can share ideas and resources. Staff are more likely to know and exchange ideas with colleagues from other departments in a small institution. This allows for both within, and across, departmental collaboration as reported by Morrison *et al.* (2003). All the six participant groups in this project have successfully completed their research work. The outcome of the six projects included two articles in peer reviewed journals, four presentations at national and international conferences and six in-College staff development seminars.

The commitment of the Fellowship project towards supporting collaborative research proved to be important; this is evidenced by the number of researchers who, despite relatively high teaching commitments, successfully carried out their projects within the specified time-frame. In considering what strategy could be used to help staff with limited experience it can be argued that the nature of collaborative research projects constitutes a catalytic force to help to bring about such a development.

Some thoughts on developing research and scholarship in small higher education institutions

The key ingredients needed for successful change management could be summarised by the following:

1 *Commitment and support from the senior management* within an institution: this finding supports the conclusions of earlier studies (see, for example, Bazeley 1994). Commitment and support needs to take a variety of forms in order to meet both financial and human resources needs. Moreover, the absence of senior management support can foster a sense of isolation in those staff who see research as an integral part of their academic work.

2 *A champion for change-management*: it became evident that a project of this nature and scale requires the leadership of a member of the academic community who is seen to possess the knowledge, skills and experience needed by the project.

3 *Overcoming staff's apprehension*: this can be achieved through the use of appropriate approaches and strategies such as the use of collaborative

research projects, on-going and available support, constant encouragement, continuous monitoring and knowledge inputs when needed.

4   *Developing enabling schemes*: these are schemes that facilitate staff research and scholarship such as time allocated for scholarship, small research grants, support with higher degrees, sabbaticals, conference attendance and staff research seminars.

5   *Planning and management*: a project of this nature requires prudent planning and effective management aimed at developing a critical mass of staff who have common research interests and who can share ideas and resources.

6   *Peer learning*: the opportunity to share processes and outcomes in a non-threatening and supportive environment.

7   *Acknowledgement of skill/knowledge capability*: the creation of appropriate partnerships that proactively bring together staff with different levels of knowledge, skills and experiences.

What helped and what went well

The participants demonstrated tremendous enthusiasm and a strong commitment towards achieving the objectives of the project. They valued the opportunity to share ideas and work collaboratively with colleagues from the same department or across a number of departments on projects of mutual interest. Giving staff the choice to negotiate a project rather than following a centrally determined research agenda proved to be important. Providing staff with the opportunity to present research seminars around their chosen topic helped to boost confidence for less experienced staff. Others were encouraged to present externally which raised the profile of the institution. Periodical seminars were organised to provide a forum for the research groups to share their findings and experience. These occasions proved to be valuable for staff development and an excellent way of forging new collaborative projects.

What hinders research and scholarship

The issues faced by Newman are similar to those of other small teaching intensive institutions. These institutions are conceived as teaching institutions and hence see themselves as having little research capacity. The barriers to developing a research culture normally include staff time/workloads, resources, support systems and structures, culture, capacity, space and infrastructure.

The most frequently identified practical restriction for non-involvement in research is that of time. However, individuals, and the institution, have sought to knit together the separate discourses of teaching and research in order to grow and nurture the research culture of the institution. A number of approaches have been used within Newman to circumvent this difficulty of time and to support staff conducting research. These included collaborative research within and across departments and re-arranging staff teaching workloads so that staff can carry a heavier load in one semester in exchange for a light load in a semester in which they wish to carry out or complete research. This helps to ensure that research is carried out bearing in mind existing resource constraints.

Recommendations

Research can be encouraged in a variety of ways. However, a mission statement that explicitly refers to the importance of developing research and scholarship combined with genuine commitment from the senior management towards research should encourage staff to embrace this aspect of their work.

Although most members of staff get involved in research and scholarship for intrinsic rewards, an effective reward system may include release time and funding support, which are two of the most requested rewards by staff, in addition to recognition by peers and leaders.

Institutions should carefully consider what constitutes appropriate research and what knowledge is included, excluded, overlooked or marginalised by these definitions of appropriate research. Members of staff need to use their own power to ensure that the developing research culture represents their values, their interests and their ways of knowing.

Medium- and long-term plans should be designed in order to ensure the continuity of such a programme. They should also link the institutional strategies for teaching and research and encourage pedagogic action and community-based research. They need to be monitored for funding and promotions.

Overview

The Fellowship project promoted research approaches through which staff could interpret demands to conduct research in ways that were congruent with their perceptions of themselves as teachers and academics. The approach aimed to assist staff to see how they could use research as an exercise of power to transform their teaching practice which they valued, rather than seeing research as something foreign and an additional burden to be resisted. The focus on pedagogical applied research has helped staff to see teaching and research as symbiotic, not antithetical. It encouraged them to research the teaching that is integral to their current identities and with which they are familiar. Applied research was a way to minimise the conflict of identity that some staff face, and to facilitate the development of a healthy research culture.

Newman has seen a significant change in engagement of staff with the research and scholarship agenda. This Fellowship has provided the time, space and impetus for staff to review their activity and to design cross-departmental projects of real worth. Indeed, there is now an increasing number of the staff who are engaged in collaborative research activity. Alongside this, there are now more opportunities available in College for supporting staff research and colleagues have a better understanding of the process of disseminating the outcome of their scholarly activities. Also, the impact of the project has also been notable because it has enabled a member of staff to demonstrate his leadership ability across the whole institution. It is hoped that the Fellowship will prove to be of lasting benefit.

References

Bass, B. and Avolio, J. (1994) *Improving Organizational Effectiveness through Trans-formational Leadership*, Sage: London.

Bazeley, P. (1994) 'From Vocational College to New University: the research profile and development needs of academic staff in a period of transition', *Higher Education Research and Development*, 13(2): 121–32.

Boyer Commission (1999) *Reinventing Undergraduate Education: A Blueprint for America's Research Universities*, Carnegie Foundation for the Advancement of Teaching: Stony Brook, New York.

Brew, A. (2001) *The Nature of Research: Inquiry in Academic Contexts*, Routledge: London.

Brew, A. (2003) 'Teaching and research: new relationships and their implications for inquiry-based teaching and learning in higher education', *Higher Education Research and Development*, 22(1): 3–18.

Durning, B. and Jenkins, A. (2005) 'Teaching/research relations in departments: the perspectives of built environment academics', *Studies in Higher Education*, 30(4): 407–26

Frank, T. (2001) 'Big-time research at small universities', *University Affairs*, April Issue.

Furrow, D. and Taylor, C. (1996) 'Research at two small Canadian universities: the views of Faculty', *The Canadian Journal of Higher Education*, 26(1): 57–73.

Jenkins, A. and Healey, M. (2005) *Institutional Strategies to Link Teaching and Research*, The Higher Education Academy: York.

Morrison, P. S., Dobbie, G. and McDonald, F. J. (2003) 'Research collaboration among university scientists', *Higher Education Research and Development*, 22(3): 275–96.

Robertson, J. and Bond, C. (2005) 'The research/teaching relation: variation in communities of inquiry', paper presented at the SRHE Annual Conference, 13–15 December, University of Edinburgh, Scotland.

Chapter 8

The cultural understanding in leadership and management (CULM) project

Phase I

Uduak Archibong and Barbara Burford

This project is enabling us to see that the future leadership of the University of Bradford might come from sources that we have neither traditionally expected nor experienced. Through CULM, we are continuing to build trust and we are creating an environment that is promoting the transcultural competence of our managers.

Professor Chris Taylor,
Vice-Chancellor and Principal,
University of Bradford

Background

Over the past ten years, many UK organisations have adopted equality and diversity policies, paving the way for increased representation of minority ethnic groups, women, disabled and mature employees in their organisations. The business case for diversity has been accepted and espoused in a variety of policy documents and reports and there is a growing body of evidence to show that the best performing organisations are also the ones that invest most in promoting equality and diversity. The UK government has played an important role in leading the way by setting clear goals that seek to ensure that public services are fully accessible and responsive to the diverse needs of all the groups and communities they serve while promoting equality and diversity in public sector employment.

An increasing number of organisations are realising that improving workforce diversity can benefit both employers and staff as well as customers and users of the organisations' outputs and/or services. Whilst the make-up of that workforce has undergone substantial changes, many organisations, the University sector included, are not truly representative of it at senior levels (AUT 2004). The lack of a representative senior management often leads to traditional working practices which have sometimes been slow to adapt to the changing nature of the modern workforce and the very changed and often well-informed expectations of customers and users.

The University of Bradford (UoB) is seeing yearly improvements in numbers of black and minority ethnic (BME) staff and students. The Corporate Plan (UoB 2004–2009) takes this further and recognises that improving diversity within the workforce and improving the working lives of staff are direct contributors to positive student learning experiences. However, unless the changes in staff and student profiles are mirrored at senior levels, the University runs the risk of missing out on the full benefits that diversity can bring.

Whilst over 18 per cent (where ethnicity is known) of UoB staff are from BME communities, only two members of staff at senior management level are from a BME background. The University has set targets and actions aimed at effectively promoting and implementing processes to address the under-representation of BME staff, particularly at middle and senior management levels and within other decision-making bodies in the University.

The cultural understanding in leadership and management (CULM) project sought to establish a diversity learning partnership scheme designed to widen the pool from which future leaders and managers within the University can be drawn in order to reflect the changing staff and student profile. The scheme aimed to harness the University's investment in race-related management development activities by linking senior white managers with middle level BME staff in a learning partnership from which both gain. This scheme differs from traditional mentoring in that learning by the more senior person is a key part of the process and differences in background and perception provide much of the basis for learning exchange. The objectives and expected outcomes of the CULM project were as follows:

Objectives

- To enable mutual learning and development in relation to equality and diversity and provide progression opportunities;
- To offer the opportunity to learn from a partner's experience and help with problem solving and change management;
- To increase confidence through support and guidance, challenging existing ideas and fostering an understanding of what each partner is 'experiencing';
- To encourage reflective practice and a 'sounding board' for ideas.

Expected outcomes

- The establishment of effective learning relationships between existing senior managers and BME staff with senior management potential;
- Raised awareness among senior University managers of the experience and perceptions of black and minority ethnic staff;
- Greater understanding by BME staff of senior management thinking – and an opportunity to influence it;

- BME staff devising and implementing career development plans which increase their suitability and likelihood of winning senior management posts.

The approach

The project used an action learning approach within a cultural competence framework (see Box 8.1). It paired together 14 senior white leaders/managers within the University with 14 senior BME academic/academic-related staff, to offer personal 'mutual' learning. A sample of senior managers was drawn from the University-wide Senior Management Committee and BME participants were drawn from the Race Equality Staff Forum. This included professors, associate dean, deputy dean and unit heads. There was careful pairing of the partners, taking into account their commitment, inter-personal skills and experience. Partners were given help and advice in understanding what was expected of them in the relationship.

Box 8.1 The project action learning framework

The project utilises an action learning framework. It consists of a ten-month programme, and will follow fundamental principles:

- Gaining commitment for the scheme
- Learning and adapting aspects of similar schemes running elsewhere
- Preparation of senior managers and BME staff for the learning partnership and the contract process
- Partnership activities over six months with a minimum of six meetings
- The continual management, monitoring and evaluation followed by full project dissemination.

This is the first phase of a project which will be rolled out to other levels of management and will create a broader, more diverse approach to developing potential leaders.

Additionally, the issues of equality and diversity remain a high profile agenda for the University, the government and other public sectors. This project will further enhance Bradford's already strong reputation for innovation and development in this area and will enable us to become a model of 'best practice' for others to learn from and follow. We will be make knowledge work for ourselves and others.

(*Source*: www.brad.ac.uk/acad/health/research/cid/culm)

Partners were expected to meet at least once a month for six months. The primary purpose of the meetings was to share perspectives on achieving and building a role as a senior manager within the university and on the role and issues of being a BME member of staff, within the same environment. All participants were required to attend regular group update meetings and two training sessions.

In deciding their approach to the relationship, the partners needed to be sensitive to each other's needs. The participants were made aware of their pre-conceptions from the outset and helped to identify ways of preventing them from having a negative impact on the learning. As it was likely that participants might partner with someone from a different gender, race/ethnicity, culture, age, sexual orientation, religion, upbringing, or any other background that may be different, it was important to be aware of different communication styles, different backgrounds and experiences, cultural differences, gender differences and stereotypes and biases.

To facilitate effective cross-cultural partnership, a survey was carried out at the beginning of the project, which looked at participants' views on the relative importance of a range of transcultural competence variables (Archibong 2002, Campinha-Bacote 1994). Attitudes to transcultural issues were ascertained using a bespoke self-administered tool adapted from Burford's transcultural competence questionnaire (Burford 1997) comprising a series of questions based around cultural awareness, cultural knowledge, ethnicity and world views, cultural skill and cultural encounters (see Box 8.2).

The main aim was to generate qualitative data to stimulate further interest in the project. It had also always been envisaged that the initial CULM project would act as pilot for a longer-term senior management development programme and this was seen in part as collecting qualitative information as a baseline for the future (see Box 8.3).

Interviews were conducted both on an individual basis and with partners on a regular basis throughout the project. In addition, an electronic survey was conducted at the end of the project.

Box 8.2 Transcultural competence

- Cultural knowledge
- Ethnicity and world views
- Cultural skills
- Cultural encounters.

Box 8.3 CULM project overview

The CULM project will establish a 'learning partnership' scheme, aimed at widening the pool from which future leaders and managers within the University can be drawn. The project will bring together senior leaders/managers within the University with BME staff, to offer personal 'mutual' learning . . .

Under the scheme, the senor manager will provide a wider perspective of the University and how to build a successful career within it. The BME staff member will provide a wider perspective on the issues relating to diversity. Both participants will give honest feedback and work to a mutual learning agenda.

(*Source*: www.brad.ac.uk/acad/health/research/cid/culm)

Findings

Self-rated transcultural attitudes

On cultural awareness, most respondents thought that it was either very important or vital to actively seek to be sensitive to, and conscious of their own interactions with other cultures and to actively seek to examine their own prejudices and biases. On cultural knowledge, most respondents thought that it was very important to instil some elements of theoretical groundwork and to access background information about different cultures. They thought that diversity training and management development programmes were very important in providing theoretical and educational information about different cultures.

Most respondents had sought information about other ethnic groups and world views. This was decided by the individual and they did not attach any particular relevance to their choice of ethnic groupings for study. In the past, European and Asian cultures were the most studied, however the choice has now shifted to Asian and Chinese. These choices were only reviewed occasionally and tended to be driven equally by the student profile, the University's strategy, and local and international demography.

When asked how important they thought it was to actively seek the knowledge and skill to factor cultural variables into appraisals, about half the respondents thought that this was very important or vital. Most respondents thought that it was very important to have direct encounters with members of different cultures. They were clear that it was important to be aware of intracultural variations, as well as gender, class and age variations.

Evaluation of the learning partnership programme

There was a great deal of commitment to the scheme, with no real difficulty in finding members from the majority ethnic group. However, because of under-representation, it was more difficult to find BME participants who were at a level to benefit realistically as true partners.

On the regularity of meeting, some partners met more frequently than proposed and others less often. Initially they were very careful and handled each other with 'kid gloves'. But the pairs that have got beyond that stage have been surprising and 'delighting' each other with the riches that they have shared. A project manager kept in touch with individuals and pairs by face-to-face meetings and, more often, by regular telephone calls. The project manager's role was to offer advice and access to resources and other experiences from around the world.

Amongst the pairs the average number of one-to-one meetings has been three, with about a third achieving five or six meetings. Many participants wanted more, but time constraints, partner disinterest, or no-fault drop out, prevented this. There was a perception of varying degrees of success. Even those who felt that their pairings had been very successful were clear that time was the major factor in limiting a more successful outcome.

BME participants felt that a key impact of the programme was one-to-one access to senior managers, and a chance to explore the business, policies and politics of the University beyond the usual meeting-driven agenda. For white participants a key impact was heightened and personalised aware-ness of the issues facing their BME colleagues, and for some there was also (self) validation and challenges of their own personal and professional practice.

Another very successful feature of the project has been the update meet-ings where people have been able to share some of their experiences and to ask questions in an increasingly open but safe environment. Towards the end of this phase experts on topics such as international leadership com-petencies and recognising and managing talent were brought in to hold half-day seminars. These were designed to enable the contextualising of learning and hasten, or make more explicit, the process of actively applying their joint learning to the work that they all do in leading the University.

For many, the best part of participation in the project has been the opportunities on many levels to take part in broad discussions in an informal context: getting to know and interact with their partner; getting to know the group without just talking about specific work issues. It was acknowledged that the CULM project had, by deliberate design, 'created a confidential and safe environment for answering awkward questions and remaining open and unconstrained about views'. Many participants felt that the 'expert seminars' were the best part of the project for enabling 'safe discussion of "wicked questions" '. It was interesting that although many participants felt that others should have access to these experts, they did not want to open the CULM seminars to non-members of the project and were quite clear that this was because they valued the environment which had been created.

Given the short time-span, we have not been as successful as we would have liked. Many pairs found it difficult to coincide diaries to meet, and given that we were aware that moving forward on such delicate and sensitive personal issues is never easy, there was a sense that sometimes this offered a perverse incentive not to prioritise meetings. Time constraints: both the short project time and lack of time to meet have been identified as amongst the worst problems with the project. However, there was also concern about the pairings and many questioned whether more consultation would not have produced better results. There was also a perception of less commitment of some participants, and certainly cynicism was expressed by some BME participants of where the true benefits lay.

Summary

As the political, social, economic and technological context in which we operate changes, we need leaders who are not only au fait with the current circumstances, but who understand each other and the communities that they serve in a deeper, more personal and experiential way. This means that their responses to future scenarios are truer and more collaborative. Their visions and ideas will also be much more imaginative and iconoclastic because of that knowledge and the lessening of fear.

CULM is about using resources that we already have to help us build leadership and talent development skills that an organisation such as ours needs now and in future. The project supported and enabled development in relation to transcultural competence and leadership, and provided opportunities that designed to help increase confidence and encourage reflective practice in both groups.

Key success factors

There were a number of factors which contributed to the success of phase 1 of this project:

- using the talents and skills of the present leadership to help their joint development further in a way that is explicit, strategic and yet intensely personal
- leadership commitment for the scheme
- using existing structures and initiatives
- learning and adapting other schemes
- preparing senior managers and BME staff for effective transcultural learning partnership

- credible project management
- open acknowledgement of fear and vulnerability
- regular group updates and meetings
- working with the pairs to build personal objectives/seeking to be constantly experiential to embed learning.

Learning points

Further to the key success factors, there were a number of learning points which resulted from the approach to change adopted by the Project Leader and Manager. Clearly, to gain lasting and embedded change takes time and thus a realistic approach to any such transition framework to bring about the required culture change needs to take account of some key learning points.

- Do not expect instant change. It will not always be possible, or politic to claim credit for changes.
- There should be no surprises, no exposures, good or bad, without explicit permission.
- Do not try to push the discussions.
- Do not expose or challenge before people are ready.

Next step

It was recognised that the approach adopted in the CULM project was just the first phase of a process which would take time if it were to bring about the deep and lasting change required. Planning for the next stages included consideration of:

- applying the lessons and practice to the whole leadership of the organisation;
- CULM to be opened to BME and white staff at other levels of management and the focus to be extended to cover gender;
- things we would do differently after this first phase of the CULM project:
  - more consultation about the pairings
  - a longer project timescale with more specific directions on development and agreement on objectives and the outcomes sought
  - planning and marketing of 'update' and 'expert' seminars.

But the foundations have been laid.

References

Archibong, U. E. (2002) 'Frameworks for anti-discriminatory strategies in the health service', in D. R. Tomlinson and W. Trew (ed.) *Equalising Opportunities, Minimising Oppression*, Routledge: London.

Association of University Teachers (AUT) (2004) *The Unequal Academy: UK Academic Staff 1995–96 to 2002–03*. Association of University Teachers: London.

Burford, B. (1997) 'Cultural competence: myth, useful concept or unattainable goal? An examination of the human resource development implications of providing healthcare in a multi-cultural community', MBA Dissertation, University of Durham.

Campinha-Bacote, J. (1994) *The Process of Competence in Health Care: A Culturally Competent Model of Care*, Transcultural C.A.R.E. Associates: Cincinnati, OH.

University of Bradford (UoB) (2005) *Corporate Strategy 2004–2009*, University of Bradford.

Chapter 9

Collaborative research across HEIs

Developing effective forms of governance, leadership and management

Kevin Edge and Patricia Gayá Wicks

Introduction

The goal of this Leadership Foundation Fellowship project was to delineate the wide range of leadership, governance and management issues associated with a 'deep'[1] collaborative enterprise and to consider the change management issues involved in facilitating and embedding strategic collaborative relationships between HEIs. This chapter presents the context, the approach to the project and the key findings and recommendations that emerged. Guidance to prospective collaborators is presented, addressing the issues and challenges that may arise in the early stages of inter-institutional collaboration.

Context

There is increasing interest in inter-institutional research collaboration across the HE sector, both in the UK and abroad. The advantages of inter-institutional research collaboration have been reviewed by the Group of Eight (Go8) universities in Australia. These eight universities receive over 70 per cent of national competitive research grants and conduct 60 per cent of all Australian university research and are engaged in a variety of collaborative activities with publicly-funded research agencies (PFRAs). In a report submitted to the Australian government (Go8 2003: 4–5), the Go8 suggest that the benefits of inter-institutional research collaborations between universities and PFRAs include:

- clearer and faster identification of research problems
- reduction in overlap, leading to greater focus of research
- cost-savings through more efficient access to and use of research infrastructure and economies of scale in purchasing power
- improved communication between key researchers
- achievement of critical mass

- more effective learning through networks
- wider experience for students
- enhanced ability to identify and recruit new staff
- new insights/innovation
- potential for greater level of research commercialisation.

The Go8 suggest that diverse modes of activity suit different objectives and desired outcomes, each of which would require particular management approaches (Go8 2003: 4–5). Forms of collaboration, listed in order of increasing formality, are summarised in Box 9.1.

The HEFCE Strategic Plan for 2003–08 (HEFCE 2005) repeatedly makes reference to collaboration amongst HEIs and other partners, advocating that this is one of a number of strategies necessary to respond to current challenges in the HE sector. The *Strategic Plan* is neither specific nor prescriptive about the forms of collaboration which are desirable; rather, it suggests that an increasingly global knowledge economy calls for 'closer collaboration between HEIs and a growing range of new and dynamic partnerships between them and potential users of their knowledge, expertise and facilities'.

Great Western Research (GWR)

The emerging GWR initiative for collaborative research between HEIs in the South West of England has been the primary case study used in the LFFP project. The vision is to catalyse strong collaboration between the regional HEIs, based around those that are more research-intensive: the Universities of Bath, Bristol and Exeter. GWR will provide high-level research training

---

Box 9.1 Forms of collaboration

Form of collaboration	Objective
Informal exchange	Sharing of knowledge, intelligence
Teaching	Exposure to/of students
PhD co-supervision	Information exchange, wider knowledge resource for student, project outcome
Access to research equipment	Enabling/facilitating research
Committee/Board membership	Provision of informed advice
Collaborative projects	Sharing inputs/outputs of research
Contracts	Purchase of research services
Formal agreements	Establishment of joint efforts, designated centres, joint ventures
IP exploitation	Mutual commercial return

for the region's most talented researchers who expect to find careers in industry-based research and development (R&D). It will promote the sustainability of research in the SW by providing mechanisms to encourage collaboration between the HEIs, business partners and government research agencies around research of international excellence.

The GWR initiative focuses on five disciplinary themes in which it is intended to develop collaborative activity. Academic staff at the Universities of Bath, Bristol and Exeter developed the academic rationales underpinning these five areas for potential collaborative development, drawing on RAE 2001 data, taking due account of areas of major importance for the SW, and analysing where the impact of any investment would be maximised and greatest value added.

The principal objectives of the initiative are:

- to ensure the sustainability of internationally excellent research in SW England by building a strong cadre of postgraduate students and post-doctoral research staff engaged in collaborative research with co-supervisors drawn from at least two HEIs;
- to catalyse the building of partnerships with major research funders;
- to establish a South West (SW) Graduate Training Network;
- to build collaborative, interdisciplinary research at the interface of existing disciplines by engaging with the South West Regional Development Agency (SWRDA) and business research teams;
- to encourage growth in business-funded Research and Development (R&D) in the South West (SW).

GWR is jointly funded by HEFCE (Strategic Development Fund), the SWRDA, and SW businesses, with a total value of £14.08 m. The GWR initiative is one strand of activity of the South West Research Alliance (SWRA) that aims to promote and build the research capacity of the South West (SW) region.

Planning

Numerous challenges arise when endeavouring to increase collaborative activity. Reflecting on his significant experience of *international* collaborative research, Pettigrew (2003: 354) poses and considers the following questions:

Do the benefits outweigh the cost? What additional intellectual, social and political skills are demanded of everyone in these kinds of knowledge production? What are the special challenges imposed on those who seek to coordinate or lead this kind of research, and how do we prepare future generations of scholars to be motivated and skilful in collaborative research?

Box 9.2 LFFP project process

1 Review of all the relevant literature and evidence
2 Conduct interviews with stakeholders of GWR to determine interest/s
3 Analyse stakeholder responses
4 Determine potential strategies to gain support and reduce obstacles.

Through the LFFP project, the various challenges and complexities that are raised through such initiatives were considered. Interviews of stakeholders of GWR and other inter-institutional collaborations were undertaken, supported by a broad-brush engagement with some of the relevant literature and the related evidence base. A stakeholder analysis was undertaken in the early stages of the project in order to identify stakeholders' interests and to consider potential strategies for gaining support or reducing obstacles (Gayá Wicks and Edge 2005: 95). The project focused on leadership, governance and management considerations, especially as experienced by those in positions of senior management (see Box 9.2).

Key themes in emerging research collaborations

As one would expect, at this stage in the development of GWR, its value as a model for inter-institutional collaboration revolves around the experiences and lessons learned in the early stages of alliance formation. Striving to successfully negotiate these initial challenges may present significant opportunities for learning. In a discussion of inter-firm learning, Mohr and Sengupta (2002: 283) suggest that 'learning about *how* to partner – the skills and procedures necessary to enhance collaborative advantage – can, in and of itself, be an important source of competitive know-how'. Attending carefully to the process of *learning how to partner* is particularly important insofar as it enhances the potential for collaborative success in the short-term and medium-term. Arguably, perceived success in the short- and medium-term could help to embed the willingness and capacity to collaborate into the future.

A key theme explored in interviews of stakeholders of GWR revolved around their aspirations for the initiative and their perceptions of how success would be manifested in relation to inter-institutional research collaboration. Six points emerged (summarised in Box 9.3) which are considered in detail below.

Box 9.3 Points arising from discussions around 'What will make for success in the initiative?'

1 Quality of relationships
2 Negotiation with funders
3 Maintaining momentum
4 Support structures
5 Managing process and outcomes
6 Addressing training and development needs.

Quality of relationships

The literature around inter-institutional collaboration by and large supports the notion that underpinning successful strategic alliances are elements of trust and shared strategic intent. At various points during the development of GWR, issues of trust, mutuality and personal relationships moved to the forefront of champions' and stakeholders' attention. A number of these instances could potentially be understood as presenting significant challenges to the leadership of GWR and to the progress of the initiative.

The idea and impetus for GWR emerged from the existing personal relationships between the Deputy-/Pro-Vice-Chancellors (D/PVCs) of the three core universities, Bath, Bristol and Exeter. The three D/PVCs, and those who worked closely alongside them in the creation of GWR, consistently state that effective personal relationships at the D/PVC level across these three universities made it possible to think about working together strategically. While the strong relations between the D/PVCs was key in providing the energy and commitment necessary to take the initiative forward, the wish to work together as a tripartite group gave rise to unintended consequences that posed a real challenge to the advancement of GWR. This surfaced in the form of other universities in the region perceiving themselves as being excluded. The challenge for the leadership of GWR was to find ways of working with the opposition to their initial, more narrowly defined vision of research collaboration, and to negotiate ways of opening this up to others while also maintaining the core of what they had envisaged for their own institutions. The proposal for GWR that was eventually approved by the funders includes a component for which all HEIs in the SW are eligible (involving opportunities for co-supervision of 130 PhD studentships that are available). It is widely acknowledged that this move enhanced the potential of GWR to advance collaborative activity and the quality of research across the region.

In seeking to form collaborative alliances, those leading the initiative need to consider how the boundaries drawn affect others with whom they have existing collegial relationships. In the HE sector, these boundaries may be particularly significant if felt to (intentionally or otherwise) amplify distinctions between those institutions that are traditionally considered more or less research-intensive. Significantly, the manner in which such prospective alliances are formulated and presented may help to ease concerns about the extent to which these favour some players to the detriment of others. It is worth pointing out that tensions may be experienced between the need to maintain goodwill, trust and collegial relations, and the wish to gain competitive advantage in a sector that is essentially competitive. A further challenge facing strategic leaders of inter-institutional collaborations, then, is that of developing trust amongst partners while continuing to operate in an environment that is necessarily and decidedly competitive.

Negotiations with funders

Another dynamic that presented both challenges and opportunities to the development of GWR was the process of negotiating and contracting with funders. Champions and representatives of other research collaborations that were contacted shared similar experiences. Two related issues emerged as needing particular attention. The first was to do with the clarity and complementarity of expectations (Parsons and Shils 1951: 15) between the funding body and the institution(s) seeking funding, and the second was to do with overcoming differences in ways of working.

The issue of clarity and complementarity of expectations is important because funding bodies have specific remits that they naturally strive to preserve and promote. In order to safeguard these remits and ensure that their objectives are being upheld, funding organisations may wish to retain varying degrees of control regarding how their funds are allocated and employed. The stakeholders and champions of the various strategic research collaborations that were contacted seemed, by and large, to agree that difficulties arose when one of the partner organisations sought greater authority and control over the process than others. This is further supported by the literature on research collaboration in the academic sector (e.g. Quinlan and Akerlind 2000).

The experiences of GWR and other strategic research collaborations suggest that actual or pursued inequity in the decision-making process can be experienced as potentially detrimental to the future success of research collaborations, since such a positioning arguably undermines the spirit of collaboration supposedly underpinning these alliances. Moreover, it is feared that unhelpful power differentials may eventually weaken and possibly jeopardise the extent to which partners are able to develop the goodwill trust and openness that, arguably, are key to the success of strategic alliances.

Funders may feel compelled to impose specific conditions in making awards, and these may be negotiable to a greater or lesser extent. Where negotiations involve a single HEI and a funding body, the degree of compromise that will or will not be acceptable is generally well understood by those representatives

Box 9.4 Learning how to partner: key skills

Key skills in learning how to partner may be seen to revolve around understanding differences and negotiating acceptable compromises amongst institutions of different types, including HEIs and funding bodies. This may require assurance that strategy and policy decisions are in alignment with the needs and expectations of all key stakeholders, and that differences in working practices, along with the prospective challenges these may bring, are recognised and successfully navigated.

engaged in the process. Negotiations involving multiple HEIs are more problematic in that what may be an acceptable compromise to one partner may be unacceptable to another. Indeed, at one stage of the development of GWR, considerable difficulties were experienced in funding negotiations, to the extent that the initiative nearly foundered. In due course, that particular challenge was successfully overcome. Nevertheless, this incident highlighted that clarity as to what constitutes a 'deal breaker' amongst all the partners is vitally important if negotiations are to be effective. Reaching a compromise that was acceptable to all was possible because the D/PVCs involved were able to establish a clear understanding of their respective Senior Management Teams' (SMTs') scope for negotiation, and were able to make this clear to one another and to the funding bodies.

Maintaining momentum

Within the context of the LFFP project, an important point to make is that those in leadership and management positions would do well to consider how they may maintain momentum at the grassroots level, even as discussions on the detail of strategy and policy are ongoing. It may be particularly imperative to avoid unnecessary loss of time and momentum when contextual pressures make swift progress at the grassroots level desirable. This is the case for GWR, where the HEIs involved wish to see the 130 studentships in place in time for the RAE 2008. Several of the stakeholders that were interviewed recognised the need for rapid response and for sustained momentum in light of perceived time pressures. They also emphasised that negotiating and contracting with industrial partners could take time, and as one senior academic put it, was 'no trivial matter'. This led to the decision to establish a Shadow Strategy and Management Board, responsible for leading GWR until the official Board is in place in order to find ways of providing a sufficiently sound framework to facilitate progress at the academic level, along a relatively tight timeline.

Support structures

The potential to overload academic support structures, such as those responsible for considering legal contracts and issues around intellectual property, has already been identified within GWR. In an interview with a member of the Research and Commercialisation Team at one of the core HEIs of GWR, it became apparent that GWR could significantly add to the workload of the team within a concentrated time period. It may be necessary to agree points of principle at the outset and restructure processes and/or provide administrative support.

A participant of the conference *Building Cross-University Alliances that Enhance Research* (Rice 1999) also identifies the management of transaction costs and additional workloads (along with the possibility for increased bureaucracy) as key challenges confronting academics working collaboratively.

Managing process, managing outcomes

The importance of finding a balance between attention to process and attention to outcomes is linked to the amount of time one may need to commit to the initial stages of forming collaborative alliances. Champions of strategic collaborations may promote such a balance by making space for potential academic collaborators to meet and develop relationships, while at the same time prompting attention to the various aspects of contracting, project management and decision-making that academics may wish to consider as they seek to form collaborative relationships with one another.

Training and development needs

The early stages of inter-institutional collaboration calls for significant skills and competencies on the part of stakeholders at all levels of the collaboration, from strategy and policy negotiations between institutions, to the management of specific research projects at the academic level. As well as communicating the value of devoting time and energy to skills development, institutional leaders should also consider how such efforts might be rewarded, and how such interventions may best be facilitated. One option might be to hold well-facilitated discussions around key topics and themes (such as relationship-building, contracting, collaborating with industry partners, and so on) as part of an 'away day' or a meeting/conference space relating to GWR (see Box 9.5).

Such gatherings may serve the multiple purposes of making space for relationship-building and inspirational encounters; focusing attention on operational and contractual requirements; and creating opportunities for skills development and explicit reflection on *learning how to partner*.

Box 9.5 Learning how to partner: suggestions for initial workshops

- Relationship-building
- Contracting
- Collaborating with industry partners.

Reflections and recommendations

Interviews undertaken as part of the LFFP project process served to encourage explicit articulation of stakeholders' aspirations and objectives for GWR. It became apparent that administrators and academics across the participating HEIs were generally in agreement that long-term research excellence was a key desired outcome. On one level, GWR was understood to present immediate opportunities for increased collaborative research activity in the short- and medium-term, through the funding of studentships and fellowships. Nevertheless, these outcomes appeared to be understood as secondary to the potential for increased research excellence in the long-term. This understanding of success as multi-layered, and as relating to short, medium- and long-term objectives, suggests that those in strategic leadership positions need to consider how success in one of these time-frames supports success at another.

The experience of GWR indicates that attention to relationships needs to be given not only at the academic collaborator level, but also at the institutional level, when SMTs and champions of prospective strategic collaborations seek to develop partnerships across and between institutions.

Strategic leaders need to appreciate that tensions may be experienced between the high premium placed on trust, and the fact that institutional partners continue to co-exist in an environment that is necessarily and essentially competitive. Finding ways to develop trust and effective partnerships in a sector that is characterised by competition is therefore a key challenge.

Box 9.6 Multi-layered success

Those in strategic management positions need to understand the different components and layers of 'success', as understood by key stakeholders and potential collaborators. They also need to consider how these tie in with one another. A multi-layered understanding of strategy may also be communicated to all stakeholders, so that there is clarity around how different components of an initiative form part of the forward strategy and potential long-term success of the institution.

Box 9.7 Personal and organisational relationships

Attention should be given to the quality of personal (and organisational) relationships amongst potential partners and that champions of such collaborations should proceed with care so as to establish and maintain goodwill trust amongst key stakeholders. Those leading strategic collaborations should be mindful of the need to strike a balance between devoting time and energy to negotiations and to relationship-building, and finding ways to move forward and maintain momentum at all levels within the initiative.

Champions must not only identify who the key stakeholders are, but also need to consider what structures and processes would need to be put in place so as to involve, appropriately, key stakeholders as plans for inter-institutional collaboration are developed. In the experience of GWR, the LFF research process was useful as an additional process for one-to-one in-depth engagement with various stakeholders. Such a process was facilitated by the appointment of a LFFP Project Officer who then took explicit responsibility for engaging in relevant interviews.

The LFFP project undertaken in parallel with GWR has been helpful in focusing attention on the competencies required at a senior leadership level, and on the kinds of management and governance structures most appropriate for responding to the specific challenges and conditions experienced. This project has also highlighted various stakeholders' perspectives regarding the competencies and skills called for at the level of academic researchers engaging in particular projects.

Box 9.8 Embedding support and incentives

Systematic attention needs to be given to the skills and capacities of academics and administrators, both in the early stages of such an initiative, and also in a continuing way as the initiative progresses. One possible solution is to work closely with Staff Development Teams within institutions, in an effort to design and offer appropriate opportunities for training and skills development. Strategic leaders of inter-institutional collaborations may not only need to communicate the importance of devoting time and energy to *learning how to partner*, but also need to consider how such efforts at the academic level may be rewarded, and how such interventions may best be facilitated.

Box 9.9 Taking account of transaction costs

Champions of inter-institutional collaborations should find ways of managing and minimising the transaction costs which emerge as the initiative progresses. This is key since senior administrators have many other responsibilities within their HEIs, as borne out in the experience of the D/PVCs of Exeter, Bristol and Bath, who took on the additional responsibility of initiating and establishing GWR. Experience with GWR supports the need for there to be individuals specifically appointed to fulfil central support and project management roles, and to take responsibility for facilitating collaborative activity across institutions.

Engagement with key stakeholders at various stages in the development of GWR has helped to give shape to the forms of management, governance and leadership which are considered to be appropriate for this initiative. It is recommended that those in leadership positions be aware of both the need to involve key stakeholders in contributing to the formation of appropriate management and governance structures, and the need to make decisions which allow progress to be made along tight time-frames, where necessary.

Overview

The goal of the LFFP project was to delineate the wide range of leadership, governance and management issues associated with a 'deep' collaborative enterprise, and to consider the change management issues involved in facilitating and embedding strategic collaborative relationships between Higher Education Institutions (HEIs). The emerging Great Western Research (GWR) project has provided the opportunity to explore and consider in some depth the various issues involved in the early stages of such an initiative, drawing on the perspectives, sense-making and unfolding understanding of a number of stakeholders. At the same time, the research process underpinning this LFFP project has also served to encourage and facilitate dialogue, systematic reflection and critical analysis by those intimately involved in GWR. This has brought with it the associated benefits of drawing attention to the issues, challenges and opportunities that arise as such initiatives progress, and to how those involved might effectively engage with and respond to these.

The work has identified the various considerations and processes involved in shaping such alliances, including the fostering and development of personal relationships, the effective identification and negotiation of opportunities and challenges, and the various skills and competencies required in constructing and facilitating such an initiative.

Note

1 Defined here as *sustained* engagement in research collaboration, embracing jointly held grants and contracts, co-supervision of research staff and joint publications, amongst others.

References

Gayá Wicks, P. and Edge, K. A. (2005) *Encouraging, Supporting and Embedding Collaborative Research Across HEIs: Developing Effective Forms of Governance, Leadership and Management*, University of Bath Report.

Group of Eight (Go8) (2003) *The Group of Eight Submission to the Review of Closer Collaboration between University and Major Publicly Funded Research Agencies*, a Group of Eight Policy document, available from http://www.go8.edu.au/policy/papers/2003/0905.htm [accessed 29 October 2005].

Higher Education Funding Council for England (HEFCE) (2005) *HEFCE Strategic Plan 2003–08*, available from http://www.hefce.ac.uk/pubs/hefce/2005/05_16/05_16.doc [accessed 29 October 2005].

Mohr, J. and Sengupta, S. (2002) 'Managing the paradox of inter-firm learning: the role of governance mechanisms', *Journal of Business and Industrial Marketing*, 17 (special issue): 282–301.

Parsons, T. and Shils, E. A. ([1951] 2001) *Toward a General Theory of Action: Theoretical Foundations for the Social Sciences*, [Harvard University Press] reprinted by Transaction Publishers: New Brunswick.

Pettigrew, A. M. (2003) 'Co-producing knowledge and the challenges of international collaborative research', in A. M. Pettigrew, R. Whittington, L. Melin *et al.* (eds) *Innovative Forms of Organizing*, Sage: London, pp. 352–74.

Quinlan, K. M. and Akerlind, G. S. (2000) 'Factors affecting departmental peer collaboration for faculty development: two cases in context', *Higher Education*, 40: 23–52.

Rice, M. L. (ed.) (1999) *A Compilation of Papers Originally Presented at a Conference Sponsored by the Merrill Advanced Studies Center: 'Building Cross-University Alliances that Enhance Research', July 1999, University of Kansas*. A Merrill Center publication, Report No. 103.

Chapter 10

The leadership succession challenge for higher education

A pilot of leadership development centres at Newcastle University

Tony Stevenson and Lynne Howlett

Context

This chapter describes Newcastle University's pilot of an approach to leadership succession management and development undertaken between January and November 2005. The work was funded by a Leadership Foundation Fellowship, and this chapter informs colleagues of the methodology, potential difficulties, benefits and lessons learned from introducing a leadership framework and a development centre approach for identifying and developing prospective Heads of School in a traditional pre-1992 university.

To execute its mission and vision the University recognised that it needed to continue to develop its leadership capability and capacity at all levels in its academic and administrative areas. Historically its leaders were selected 'papally' using soundings from school/faculty members and a nomination system where appointments were often made without interviews. A restructuring exercise in 2001 led to the University moving towards more comprehensive job descriptions and person specifications and, in a more systematic way, appointing leaders with the right mix of skills and experience through applications and interviews. The pool of applicants was small and any leadership and management development generally took place once the leader was in post. Newcastle University was not alone in this. A 2005 Leadership Forecast Survey reported only 21 per cent of UK organisations fill leadership positions internally.

Succession management and development for leaders at Newcastle University had been less systematic than it might have been and given increasing pressures on leaders across the University it was recognised that identifying and developing a 'pool' of potential leaders ahead of appointment was necessary. Over the three years to 2007/8 Newcastle, with a system of rotating headships, anticipated that it may need to identify around 20 new Heads of School. This chapter describes a project which the University undertook to help address some of these succession difficulties.

The chapter describes how through a development centre pilot the University introduced a process which helped identify prospective academic leaders and developed them to be ready for more senior roles. It enabled the University to develop 'internal talent' and provided the opportunity to make leadership a more attractive option. It allowed senior managers to evaluate an individual's readiness to take on leadership roles and to support them to achieve increasingly ambitious business goals.

The pilot, which was broadly about succession planning for academic leadership roles, introduced the concept of a leadership framework (hereafter known as the Heads of School Framework) and the development centre. Although there is little evidence of these techniques being used widely in HE, they have been used extensively outside the sector and have had a significant impact on succession planning in the NHS, Primary Care Trusts, school leadership and in a range of blue chip companies including the Royal Bank of Scotland and Bayer. The culture, especially in 'old' universities with rotational leadership roles, may have hampered progress and the pressures on the system to grow our own talent were seen to be increasing. The aim was to create a 'pool' of more skilled and self-aware applicants whilst at the same time respecting diversity issues.

The scope of the project, if it were to cover all leaders in the University, was unmanageable, so work began where the need was most pressing with prospective Heads of School. To further limit the scope of the project, development centres were piloted for prospective Heads of School in the Faculty of Humanities and Social Sciences (HASS).

The following definition of a development centre was used: 'A Development Centre is the use of assessment centre technology for the identification of individual strengths and weaknesses to diagnose development needs that will facilitate more effective job performance/career advancement which in turn contributes to the greater organisational success' (Ballantyne and Povah 2004: 142).

Some of the distinguishing features of a development centre are:

- it is not a pass/fail event
- participants 'own' their results/data
- feedback occurs during and after the centre
- reflection and development starts at the centre
- focus is on criteria that can be developed
- pre- and post-centre activities are the norm.

The University's intention was that unlike assessment centres for job applicants where the centre is the end of the process, the development centre would be the start of the development process. Table 10.1 shows the difference between a development centre and an assessment centre (Ballantyne and Povah 2004: 142).

The approach used at Newcastle is a third generation development centre.

Table 10.1 Development centres vs. assessment centres

Assessment centre	Development centre		
Selection	Identify potential	Diagnostic approach	Coach and develop
External recruitment Internal promotion	Fast-track Hi-potentials Succession planning	Define needs against existing and new values and behaviours	Address needs to aid culture change and encourage new values and behaviours
Assessors assess behaviour and select	Assessor/observers assess behaviour and define gaps against more senior job	Observers assess behaviour and define gaps against current job	Observer/coach changes behaviour Close gaps within current job

Table 10.2 Evolution of development centres

Centre type	First generation	Second generation	Third generation
Participant involvement	Minimal – participants simply tackle exercises	Feedback to participants at end of centre, sometimes after each exercise	Joint decision-making on competencies displayed after each exercise
Exercises and tests	Off-the-shelf exercises and psychological tests	Mainly off-the-shelf exercises and psychological tests	Mainly real-life business problems
Development planning	Little – perhaps part of post-centre feedback	Sometimes given on the centre to planning, with monitoring and support afterwards	More time given on the centre with significant monitoring and mentoring afterwards

With third generation centres there is a greater opportunity for self and peer assessment. This often results in a greater commitment to the personal development plans since participants have helped to define the development needs and appropriate actions. Table 10.2 shows the evolution of development centre design up to the third generation of the 1990s.

Newcastle University's development centre took the format illustrated in Box 10.1.

Communication about the pilot

It was critical to engage the University's senior management, starting with the Vice-Chancellor, at the earliest stages and to get their support for this new approach to leadership succession management. The Fellowship allowed the

Box 10.1 Newcastle University's development centre

Preparation event

Welcome and introductions: Faculty PVC

- Background/context
- Leadership succession issues at Newcastle University

Individual introductions

Participants and facilitators alternately – all to include hopes and concerns regarding the event

The programme

- Explain in detail the structure of the development centre
- How to contribute/safe environment/not pass/fail, etc.
- Confidentiality

Paper-based activities

- Participants to complete in-basket exercise (1½ hours)

Lunch

Paper-based activities (continued)

- 16PF (personality questionnaire)
- Myers Briggs Type Indicator (personality questionnaire)
- Watson-Glaser Critical Thinking questionnaire
- AMT – Numerical Analysis questionnaire

In real-life

- Two experienced Heads of School provide their own descriptions of the realities of operating as a Head of School
- Question and answer session

Development centre day

Welcome back and brief discussion about yesterday

Development centre exercises

- Observed one-to-one challenging/difficult interview exercise (one hour)

- Discussions re participant's thinking around yesterday's in-basket exercise (one hour)
- Feedback re personality and psychometric questionnaire from yesterday
- Observed group discussion (one hour)

How was it for you?

- 10–15 minute discussion for participants and facilitators about the process and how it felt

Next steps

Leadership and Management Development Adviser describes what will happen next

- Describe series of subsequent meeting
- Assure confidentiality/benefits/offers on help, etc.
- Handout Leadership Development Plan

Final word: Faculty PVC

- PVC's summary, observations regarding development centre
- Goodbye, thanks and good luck to participants

Facilitators' 'wash-up' session (3–4 hours)

- Each participant is rated and discussed at length
- Evidence-based reports are produced for each participant to be fedback in 1–2-hour meetings

University to invest financially in the development of the Heads of School framework, the training of in-house observers and the running of the development centre.

A decision was taken to buy in expertise and the consultants (occupational psychologists) were selected because they had previously provided assessment centres to fill leadership and senior academic vacancies within the University and were aware of the cultural norms and complexities of HE. They had much experience of leadership frameworks and development centres and worked closely with the Project Manager throughout. The plan was always to develop University leaders as in-house development centre 'observers' with the aim of eventually reducing the reliance on the consultants.

Effective early communication was essential. The Vice-Chancellor and three Faculty Pro-Vice-Chancellors were consulted and other members of the University's Executive Board either received copies of the bid or attended presentations by the PVC who held the LFFP Fellowship, who at the time was HASS Faculty Pro-Vice-Chancellor. He had the necessary influence and authority and now the financial resource to promote the introduction of the Heads of School framework and development centre approach. In this role and in his capacity as a member of the Staff Committee and Executive Board he also had influence at University level.

All initial communications, although prepared by the Project Manager, were approved and circulated under the Fellow's name to achieve greater 'buy-in'. Messages about the pilot were posted on Faculty and Staff Development mailbases and websites, an article placed in the University's staff newsletter and a point made of publicly celebrating the Leadership Foundation Fellowship.

Designing the Heads of School framework

It was important to interview a large number of leaders, especially current Heads of School, if the framework was to be accurate and owned by the people who would eventually use it. The interviews were extended beyond HASS since it had to be applicable for eventual use with all prospective Heads of School across all three Faculties.

Twenty-four University leaders were interviewed including the Vice-Chancellor, all three Faculty Pro-Vice-Chancellors and a selection of other Pro-Vice-Chancellors. These 'visionary' interviews focused on the evolving role of the Head of School and the skills and behaviours required as the role develops. The three Faculty PVCs and some of their Deans had 'repertory grid' interviews where they were asked to compare leadership behaviours and skills and explore what makes an 'outstanding' Head of School.

Each HASS Head of School was invited to a one-to-one 'critical incident' interview in which they were asked to describe specific times/situations where they had worked successfully/less successfully and the behaviours they had employed, which had worked and which had not. To ensure that the data produced was not focused too heavily on HASS, a selection of Heads of School from the other two Faculties were included.

Finally, two focus groups were held with 17 support staff, chosen at random, who reported through to Heads of School. This included lecturers, administrators, clerical staff and technicians. These informal groups discussed and recorded the effective behaviours of 'ideal' Heads of School and produced some rich and valuable data. The communication around all of these interviews was carefully disseminated, and always approved and signed off by the LFFP Fellow to encourage additional engagement.

Within a few weeks, the first draft of a Heads of School framework was produced and circulated to every person who had been interviewed. Their subsequent feedback and comments were taken into account and allowed the occupational psychologists to produce further drafts with more face validity for those who would eventually be using the framework. A user-friendly Heads of School framework was agreed (Table 10.3).

Designing and planning the development centre

Once the Heads of School framework was agreed it became possible to plan the development centre. The framework provided the basis against which a participant's performance could be measured. A range of activities were agreed to allow the observers to 'benchmark' participants against the role of Head of School and against the eight areas of the Heads of School framework.

A pre-centre 'preparation event' was planned where participants worked individually on a complex in-basket exercise and did two psychometric tests, a critical reasoning and a numerical reasoning test. They also completed two personality questionnaires. Results from this event were fedback, referenced against the Heads of School framework and used as part of the development centre.

The development centre was a one-day series of group exercises, individual role plays and group discussions around the results/data produced by each individual at the preparation event. The aim was to create a safe environment for participants to experiment with new ideas and skills and where all observation data was shared with and owned by the participants.

Beyond the development centre a supportive process which for each participant involved meetings with the Project Manager in her capacity as the University's Leadership and Management Development Adviser, the Faculty Pro-Vice-Chancellor and ongoing Performance and Development Reviews with the respective Head of School were also arranged and monitored.

Development centre 'observers'

The next step in the design process was to identify and train existing well-regarded University leaders as development centre observers. It was important, for the eventual cascading of the approach, to train observers from all three Faculties and not to simply focus on the HASS Faculty. For sustainability, Staff Developers and Human Resources Officers were included. Thirteen potential observers were invited by the Vice-Chancellor to undergo two days of intensive training and to become part of a pool from which observers for future development centres could be selected. It was important to select respected observers who would publicly value the development centre approach and who showed natural skills at recognising behaviours and feeding back, giving praise and sharing some quite sensitive behavioural evidence/issues. Research findings about the development of in-house observers were confirmed at Newcastle, for example: 'The fact that assessor/observers feel and express the need for more guidance and practice in the skills to do the

Table 10.3 University of Newcastle: Heads of School framework

Behaviour	Indicators
Working at strategic level	Sees the 'big picture' and thinks strategically; is able to manage complex problems and issues
	Able to articulate strategic vision for organisation Identifies opportunities for enhancing reputation, kudos and financial security of organisation Identifies appropriate structures for making strategic vision a reality Comfortable working with complexities Can apply numerical problem-solving skills
Leadership	Takes control to ensure that objectives are met
	Provides clear direction to others Delegates tasks to others without relinquishing control and responsibility Is comfortable with conflict and prepared to confront individuals who stand in the way of organisational achievements Acts decisively
Credibility	Inspires the trust and confidence of others by the way they handle themselves and others
	Energises others Possesses insight, particularly into the needs and motivations of others Self-confident in manner and able to take unpopular decisions Is straightforward, open and fair in dealings with others Motivated to set individual interests aside and work hard for future success of organisation
Communicating with others	Communicates with colleagues effectively; is able to persuade and influence others
	Listens to the views and opinions of others Disseminates key messages to others Is able to influence by persuasive and articulate communications Responds to communications from others in clear, appropriate and timely fashion
Working with people	Exceptional interpersonal skills
	Able to relate well to all types of people Able to alter style depending on people or situation Behaves with diplomacy Interested in others and motivated by helping them to feel valued and to succeed Motivates others so that they wish to contribute
Embraces change	Recognises the need for change and is forward-looking; promotes the benefits of change to others; is proactive in ideas generation

Behaviour	Indicators
	Accepts the reality and requirements of change Uses initiative and presents new ideas and approaches Is able to achieve change at individual and organisational level Is supportive of others during change
Planning and organising	Manages time and resources by prioritising and organising effectively
	Effective at organising and managing heavy workload Anticipates future demands for staff, information, etc. Identifies quickly what is important and prioritises and acts accordingly
Management of pressure	Copes with criticism and the demands of the job
	Is able to separate him/herself from the job in hand so that negative feedback does not become overwhelming Able to bounce back in the face of setbacks Driven to succeed even when problems seem intractable Remains positive and optimistic when going gets tough

job confirms that stimulating assessor development is another major benefit of Development Centres' (Lee 2000: 11).

In addition, Goodge found a statistically significant relationship between managerial involvement (in development centres) and improved competence and performance (Goodge 2004).

Observers at Newcastle claimed they were stretched and found the process challenging. Many spoke of how it had developed them personally as leaders and managers of others – a genuine and unexpected benefit.

Development centres: the application process

Encouraging applicants to apply to attend the development centre was carefully managed. It was important to reach academics who had an interest in finding out more about themselves and the possibility of moving into a leadership role in the future. It was essential to be clear about the purpose of the development centre so that applicants could self-select and also to publish selection criteria in the event of having too many applicants and needing to shortlist. An advertisement and an application form were posted on both Faculty and Staff Development Unit websites and mailbases. Current Heads of School were asked to encourage capable but 'reluctant' applicants and an article was placed in the University's staff newsletter. Within two weeks 14 applications had been received for the first development centre.

A selection panel of the Fellow, the Director of Human Resources and the Project Manager met to discuss the applications against the agreed criteria and the applications were reduced to 12. The standard of applications varied but all were interesting and met most of the selection criteria so even the two who did not achieve a place on the first development centre were held in reserve for the second centre. As this was a pilot it was important to make the development centre attractive and not to have to reject applicants unless necessary. Communication around the application/selection process was carefully handled and success celebrated.

Once the date of the preparation event and the development centre itself were announced and the participant's availability had been checked, the development centre participant numbers fell to six which was ideal for a manageable first development centre. There was not the same fall-out rate for the observers and a number of them subsequently did not get a chance to use their new skills at the earliest opportunity. These observers were then selected as a priority to run the next development centre.

Feedback from the development centre, from both the participants and the observers was resoundingly positive. The detailed planning, scheduling and communicating ahead of the event paid off as administratively both events ran smoothly. Energy levels and support for the process were high. The development centre approach proved to be quite revealing and can be both exposing and intimidating for participants. Confidentiality of scores, feedback etc. had to be carefully handled. However, the skill of the observers and the occupational psychologists ensured that a safe environment was created where development rather than success was key. There was also a strong emphasis on the centre not being a pass or fail event. The only requirement was that self reflection and personal development were paramount.

Participants found both events challenging, if at times, rather stressful. They claimed they were glad for the opportunity to reflect on their leadership and management styles and their potential fit with future roles. For some the development centre and feedback sessions reinforced their determination to progress in their leadership roles/careers. For others, it helped them to recognise that they would prefer to concentrate on their research careers. The centre had been invaluable in giving staff the space to think about the types of future roles they would be most suited to and happiest in. It was agreed that this increase in self awareness was important and that if, as a result of the development centre, individuals chose to focus on being more entrepreneurial or to dedicate themselves to research excellence this was as much a positive outcome as identifying a potential Head of School.

All participants recognised and valued the investment that the University had made in them. Their constructive feedback tended to be more about the administration of the centre/tests than the actual development centre process which was well received and seen to be both systematic and objective. They were very keen to stress that the less you can make a development centre feel like an assessment centre for recruitment purposes, the better. By providing a truly supportive and safe environment we are more likely to see participants opening up honestly and more fully to their development needs/opportunities.

Observers were fully aware of how challenging the process would be for them. The requirement to be objective, analytical and effective at recording evidence was understood, but until people have been through a development centre it is hard to explain how tiring it will be.

Post development centre activities

Development centres are the start of a much longer development process and the first step after the centre was for the participants to have a one-to-one feedback session with an observer based around the Head of School framework and development centre feedback report form. They then produced a leadership development plan which required them to reflect on their learning from the event and how they might identify and fill their development gaps. Support with this was provided primarily by the Leadership and Management Development Adviser and the current Heads of School. The Faculty PVC facilitated discussions with each participant individually about creative ways of ensuring more challenging work, development opportunities and career options.

Leadership development plans produced significant outputs including requests for instance to be exposed to new areas of work and mentoring with senior leaders to learn more about thinking strategically. Specific leadership development needs included:

- financial/budget awareness
- planning and organising to achieve goals
- handling conflict
- delegating and 'letting go'
- managing and prioritising an increasing workload
- thinking more broadly about Faculty/University/sector issues
- strategic 'visioning' skills
- assertiveness with challenging colleagues
- leading others through change
- decision making to make progress
- staying focused and positive in face of challenge and pressure.

Participants subsequently engaged in a range of activities including 360° feedback, one-to-one coaching, IT training, a university funding workshop and the occasional external programme. Which development activities they undertook depended entirely on their specific needs and learning styles. All, however, continue to have a formal annual performance appraisal with a six-month review. They also meet with the Leadership and Management Development Adviser every six months to check progress against their leadership development plan.

What helped?

The following list highlights things that are believed to have helped the pilot to be a success:

- Public commitment from the VC and PVCs was instrumental to the success of this pilot and has proved to be essential in the extended roll-out. Faculty PVCs and the Registrar have a critical role as sponsors in supporting the approach as it is introduced into each of their areas. Letters, invitation and presentations from these most senior managers had far more impact than if they had been delivered by the Staff Development Unit. They were effective in achieving 'buy-in' and in continuing to demonstrate senior management commitment to and engagement in the process.
- Committed and skilled University 'observers/facilitators' were critical to the pilot. They demonstrated University-level support for the process. Additionally their understanding of the leadership culture proved to be essential for observing and recording behaviour, and especially for the feedback sessions with the participants.
- Senior managers, recognising the impact on the business if they did not develop leaders for the next five to ten years, generated the energy for this challenging pilot.
- It became clear that significant financial investment at the outset is often justified in the payback. For example, in this case investing early can prevent expensive mistakes in the Heads of School appointment process. It was calculated that to run a Development Centre costs 0.0001 per cent of Newcastle University's total income. The waiting lists for current development centres are most encouraging and the future will focus less on the Head of School role and more on generic leadership skills for a range of leadership roles.
- It became very clear during the pilot that the development centre process is unlike anything these prospective academic leaders had experienced before and that a clear supportive briefing was essential. Mandatory briefing sessions are now part of the process to ensure that participants are sure about what they are undertaking. During the pilot the briefing sessions were voluntary, not frequently taken up and as a result participants were less well prepared than they might have been.
- A dedicated and skilled Project Manager that understood the culture was essential to drive this potentially sensitive process forward. Although consultant expertise was used, a University Project Manager will always

be needed to handle all in-house communication between participants, Heads of School, the consultants and University observers.

- Planning well in advance is critical. Six- to twelve-month lead times allow for effective planning and diary management for very senior managers acting as observers and for the participants themselves.
- The one-and-a-half separate days of the first pilot were disjointed and the development centres are now run over a one-and-a-half consecutive day event to improve group cohesion.
- The development centre process can be quite exposing/intimidating unless handled with extreme care. It was essential to put a great deal of emphasis on the opportunity for 'development in a safe environment' as opposed to 'assessment'.
- Assuring confidentially of the data/documentation produced at the centre and clarity regarding other Human Resources processes (for example, annual appraisal or promotions) was essential and guidelines proved to be helpful for both participants and observers.

Results of the pilot

A very positive result from the pilot was that a leadership/Heads of School framework was successfully launched and embraced into a pre-1992 University with very little resistance. Subsequent work sees the University moving away from a specific Heads of School framework towards a single generic leadership framework which will provide a more coherent and consistent approach for use with all levels of leaders across the University. In the longer term, University leaders will be selected, developed and appraised around a generic behavioural leadership framework which they have designed themselves. It is recognised that the emergent and more generic leadership framework will be refined and continually developed as the demands on leaders evolve.

As a direct result of the development centres Newcastle University has run to date, it now has ten individuals seriously developing leadership as a central part of their careers. One has already been promoted to Head of School. Others are undergoing coaching, more self-awareness activities and attending sessions about the broader University. Some are engaged in more challenging work and two have been promoted to lead in programme/ research areas.

The process created an opportunity to involve some of the University's most senior managers in the development and succession of less senior managers. Some areas of the University are subsequently taking their succession issues more seriously and creating more supportive and developmental environments for their aspiring leaders.

The response to the pilot has been so positive that research is underway to explore the application of the framework and development centres with others groups, e.g. Principal Investigator Researchers and Senior Services Managers. There is agreement that the focus should not continue to be solely on the role of Head of School. Leadership vacancies arise throughout the University at different levels and all areas and it is believed that development centres can be used to identify and develop prospective research leaders, Deans, PVCs and leaders of services such as careers and welfare. It is likely that the University will move towards using 'fourth generation' development centres, an approach which was described by Andrew Constable (1994, cited in Ballantyne and Povah 2004: 143) at Roffey Park Management Institute. Such centres are more 'peer'-centred and include:

- peer feedback and coaching after each exercise;
- integration of off-the-shelf tests and exercises, real-life problems and activities to identify not just behaviour but values too;
- personal and group planning at the centre with even greater emphasis on follow-up, for example, through mentoring and the use of learning sets.

The University's Staff Committee has supported and continues to promote the use of these more systematic approaches to leadership development and has provided central funding to deliver them. The current waiting lists are healthy and two further Faculties plus the University's Central Services await launches in their areas over a two-year period.

Key learning

This Leadership Foundation Fellowship pilot of development centres provided three key lessons:

1   The public involvement of senior managers was critical to the success of this pilot. Early communications from the VC and the constant support of a PVC throughout the whole process was instrumental. The key learning is about having an influential sponsor when embarking on a significant change management project like this one.
2   Avoiding assumptions like 'it will never work here' and 'academics won't buy it' is critical. The learning is that success is possible if there is sufficient energy and goodwill from the key people and if the research is seen to be extensive and the consultation sufficiently far reaching.
3   Linking leadership frameworks and development centres to other Human Resource processes, e.g. leadership recruitment and performance appraisal is important. Building the framework into such processes is essential to reinforce and develop the skills of the University's more effective leaders and to provide a tool to manage the under-performance of others. Further plans include the design of a 360° feedback tool around the framework thus ensuring a more consistent approach to 360°

feedback activities and one which supports the University's views on how its leaders should be leading.

Overview

Newcastle University is not alone in its attempts to address its leadership succession challenges. The development centre process described here appears to have provided the institution with a systematic tool to identify and develop leaders of the future. Plans are in place for development centres to be used more widely across the whole institution for a whole range of leadership roles.

The next challenge is to monitor the medium-term impact of development centres, to assess whether they help to develop leaders and managers with the skill set required to lead in higher education in the next five to ten years. A good measure of success will be if these leaders go on to develop their own successors!

References

Ballantyne, I. and Povah, N. (2004) *Assessment and Development Centres*, Gower: Aldershot.

Goodge, P. (2004) 'Twenty great development centre ideas' *Selection and Development Review*, 20: 14.

Hope, K. (2005) 'Leading edge', *People Management*, 11: 16–17.

Lee, G. (2000) 'The state of the art in development centres', *Selection and Development Review*, 16: 11.

Part 3

Capacity-building to lead and manage change

Chapter 11

Towards a learning organisation
Innovation in professional discourse

Paul Gentle

This chapter aims to explore the ways in which specific interventions, including the use of action learning, coaching and institutional *Change Academy* events, might be used to bring about cultural change in the management of higher education institutions. While sited in a relatively small college of higher education (the College of St Mark and St John), the findings may also be applicable to larger institutions, particularly at the level of faculties or big departments.

Although the initial LFHE Fellowship project was built around the specific strategic challenge of increasing institutional engagement with business and community organisations, and was led by a middle manager in the College, the intention was always to ensure that lessons learnt could be transferred to other key objectives which were also contained in the College Strategic Plan.

This chapter will outline how the concept of the *learning organisation* came to be interpreted by academic staff across the institution as a result of the interventions which were funded by the project.

It will attempt to demonstrate how a focus on creating innovative approaches and settings in which professional discourse could flourish led to a broad perception of a strategically-led 'change project' which would impact on the working culture of the institution. As a result, some surprising outcomes resulted, feeding into the core academic direction of the institution, and in particular its learning and teaching strategy and curriculum offering. The potential for impact on the student learning experience of 'learning organisation thinking' was therefore more direct, and more immediate, than had been imagined when the project was conceived.

Finally, it will conclude with recommendations as to actions which could be taken by senior leaders in other institutions with an interest in aligning their cultures, and behaviours, more closely with the principles underpinning organisational learning.

Learning organisations and higher education

The project provided an opportunity to test some of the hypotheses advocated by Revans (1983), Senge (1990), Pedler (1996), McGill and Brockbank (2004) and Garrett (2001) in their explorations of experiential learning, including action learning, as instrumental to the development of learning organisations – entities which are able to improve themselves continually through systemic learning.

Senge identifies teams as 'the key learning unit in organisations' (1990: 236). This was important for the project, since its design was based on creating networks within the institution in which group learning would be crucial. In some cases, this envisaged working within existing academic units (such as subject teams or academic schools), but there was also the expectation that thematic learning would occur, based around shared interests in particular sectors (such as public policy on sports and leisure) or in non subject-specific fields such as leadership development.

Senge further stresses the importance of teams mastering discourse, characterised as 'the practices of dialogue and discussion' (1990: 237). His definition of dialogue as a process of listening and exploring while suspending views or judgement is very similar to the way in which action learning set discourse is characterised by Revans's notion of questioning insight (1983: 28). Such practices are not always manifest in the management of activity in higher education institutions, even when they form part of the set of expectations which a university or college may hold in relation to student learning.

For Senge, openness is an aspiration for organisations, mirroring the Revans idea of honesty. He distinguishes genuine openness from 'the curious phenomenon of "open closedness", when everyone feels he (*sic*) has a right to air his (*sic*) views, yet no-one really listens and reflects' (1990: 279).

Ramsden (1998) claims that effective benchmarking against good practice might result in effective departments where cooperative working is used as a means for continuous improvement. This supports a key notion underpinning the project, that new working practices might transfer to the institutional culture beyond the narrow thematic concerns of the funded activity itself.

With the public funding support of organisations such as the Leadership Foundation for Higher Education (LFHE) and the Higher Education Academy (HEA), the last few years have seen the emergence of web-disseminated literature which aims to distribute thinking and practice on change management in higher education.

Trowler *et al.*, for instance, draw on a range of theoretical models of change to consider their implications for practice (2003: 7). They also provide the helpful observation for the Fellowship project, that: 'While it is common to try and change people's thinking, we see a lot of value in using tools and expertise to change practices: beliefs can follow' (2003: 21). One of the outputs of the project was the production of a web-based toolkit of resources for supporting change activity across the institution. The project did not expect to rely on an 'evangelical' approach in order to demonstrate its value – it rather sought to model a range of practices upon which academic staff could feel free to improvise and customise to their own disciplines.

McCaffery (2004) devotes considerable space to departmental leadership, performance management, managing change and developing staff. Although there is a useful summary of the concept of the learning organisation, and recognition that HEIs do not embody this concept, there is only passing reference in the book to interventions such as coaching and mentoring, and action learning or action research are mentioned nowhere in the text. This contrasts significantly with the policy-driven literature surrounding the National College for School Leadership (NCSL), which emphasises strongly the role of the practitioner-researcher in the schools sector.

McCaffery is both helpful and original in identifying the stages of development of departmental management teams (2004: 126), in providing a typology of staff development activity (2004: 188) and in defining 'university innovators', who 'show that it is possible for institutions of learning to become more like "learning organisations"' (2004: 241). He situates this within a typology of institutional cultures, including the 'enterprise university', which is clearly the sort of culture which the Principal of the College of St Mark and St John envisaged on taking up his appointment in 2003, and which underpinned his endorsement of the application for the Fellowship.

One of the most illuminating recent texts (Sheffield Hallam University 2003) is published under the auspices of HEFCE, which supported its development through its Good Management Practice Fund. *Organisational Learning and the Future of Higher Education* is critical of the political and economic forces which have impacted on the sector's failure in not 'contributing much to the transformation required for a learning society' (2003: 3) which was highlighted in the 1997 report by the National Enquiry into Higher Education.

The primary research underpinning the above report also confirms that the Fellowship project, in seeking to transform aspects of the institutional culture in which it was based, may also be helpful to the sector as a whole: 'The responses ... collectively confirmed the view that, despite all the participative structures that characterise most universities, there was no significant evidence ... that they inspire very much real open dialogue, reflection, genuine participation or sharing other than at a superficial level' (2003: 18).

Rowley applies theory on learning organisations to the higher education context, concluding that 'the creation of a learning organisation is dependent on embedding learning in the management process of the organisation by extending the focus on learning from the classroom and research laboratory to the wider organisation' (1998: 16). Acknowledgement of this concept led to a conscious strategy for the project of modelling new management processes for the institution. The internal Change Academy, which introduced practices of improving team-based communication, of coaching and of action learning to participating teams, was an essential vehicle for the realisation of the project.

The LFHE asserts that leading change is one of the greatest challenges for leaders in higher education, pointing to some factors relevant to the Fellowship project: 'Change by its very nature generates a lot of negative energy inside organisations, and the key skill is to work with the multitude of communities within an institution to turn that . . . into something that is positive and focused' (2005: 9). It was possible that not all senior managers in the College would necessarily welcome the approaches used by the project. In some ways, in seeking to enhance devolved leadership and decision-making amongst academic teams, the project could be seen as a threat to the existing mechanisms of accountability and hierarchical authority. There was also a risk that negative energy might result from expectations raised too high in the minds of academic staff for change which could not be delivered in practice.

McGill and Brockbank caution the would-be change leader that 'Transformational as opposed to instrumental change (for improvement) at organizational levels is more aspirational than a practical reality' (2004: 47). Retaining a balanced perspective on expectations for cultural change would therefore be of great importance for the project.

Hannan and Silver (2000) address the relative impact of change which they categorise as top-down, bottom-up or middle-out. The last of these categories is arguably the most effective (and represents most closely the approach of the project) in that it involves building capacity at middle levels of the institution – departmental and team levels – which 'then reaches out and draws in policy priorities with which the department or team then engages. Innovation comes from the engagement and the capacity' (Trowler *et al.* 2003: 9).

Planning the project

The application for the Fellowship followed swiftly from a successful team experience at the first national joint LFHE and HEA Change Academy event in Edinburgh in September 2004 (see Box 11.1). This made a strong initial impact on the College, given the Principal's direct involvement as a team member. The four team members responded in varied ways to the four-day residential experience.

For the eventual Fellowship-holder, the greatest interest lay in the team-working process and the modelling of a range of techniques in support of creativity and innovation in leading change. Other team members were highly task-focused, and appeared less interested in the processes of group working or ideas generation. All members agreed that the opportunity to work in a sustained manner away from desks, e-mail and telephones represented an

Box 11.1 The Change Academy

This four-day event helps teams from higher education institutions develop the knowledge, capacity and enthusiasm for achieving complex institutional change. It provides unique opportunities for team-based learning and professional development that focus on the strategic interests and needs of the participating institutions.

Underpinning philosophy of Change Academy

Team-based working and learning are central to the Change Academy experience. This reflects a belief that the planning and implementation of complex institutional change is a collective enterprise requiring a team-based approach. The teams participating in Change Academy will vary in size and composition, they may or may not fully represent the team involved in the institutional change process but as a minimum they should represent the key individuals who will lead, coordinate and facilitate institutional change.

Teams are expected to contain between four and seven people and that where appropriate they will include a student representative. Teams will contain a mix of managers and academics with change agent roles, as well as administrative support staff, staff and educational developers, researchers, students and staff involved in guidance or providing services for students. The mix of people will reflect the particular needs of the project.

Effective leadership is crucial to the success of major institutional change projects. The Change Academy process creates situations where people have to take responsibility for leading discussion. It creates a network to support team leaders and help grow deeper understandings of how complex change is led and accomplished in higher education institutions.

A developing knowledge base – a declared aim of the Change Academy is to develop an evidence base to inform the content of the programme. Research being undertaken with the 2004 Change Academy teams, aimed at understanding how institutions accomplish complex change, will be drawn upon in the 2005 event.

The event includes:

- team-based discussions focused on different dimensions of project planning and implementation;
- plenary sessions aimed at understanding how people and organisations change and how change is evaluated;
- creative thinking sessions to help teams think about the sorts of

changes they are promoting and the particular contexts in which they work;

- social interaction and networking with other participants.

The Change Academy provides:

- a unique high quality environment for professional learning
- top class facilitation and consultancy
- support for the change process before and after the four-day residential event, including a long-term support network
- collaborative learning across institutions and the potential for networking that will have longer term unanticipated benefits
- access to the results into institutional change as it is developed through the Change Academy
- access to a wide range of relevant resources and evaluation tools.

Source: www.lfhe.ac.uk/supportteam/academy

invaluable slice of 'quality time', and many ideas materialised which later became translated into effective action back in the institution.

One of the impressive outcomes for the College was that the Principal became committed to sustaining change processes as a means to continuous institutional improvement, and was pro-active in ensuring that the College was represented at the subsequent 2005 Change Academy, and that the College's own Change Academy, in September 2005, should be a key feature of the LFHE Fellowship project.

There were several other factors which made the project of key importance to the College:

- The institution's Strategic Plan identified a commitment to regional engagement as one of 12 key objectives, and the project addressed this specifically.
- A poor track record with HEFCE for delivering on 'third leg' activity meant that the stakes for the project were high, and that strong impact was expected by the Principal.
- The sense of unfulfilled potential among academic staff which resulted from a long-established teaching-led mission in which the development and application of research with partners from business and the community had not previously been seen as a priority.
- There was a complementary development of a new research strategy, with an emphasis on applied research, including consultancy and training activity.
- The applicant had been recently appointed to a strategic role, as the institution's Director of Regional Affairs (0.3 full-time equivalent post).

Inspiration was also available from other sectors of public education, in the form of printed materials and the experiences of the National College for School Leadership (NCSL) and the post–16 sector's Centre for Excellence in Leadership (CEL). Each offers alternative sets of propositions for effective leadership from those advocated by LFHE, but both are fundamentally concerned with supporting continuous improvement in learner achievement through the engagement by teaching staff in evidence-based research, and through distribution of leadership responsibility within educational institutions.

Of particular relevance was NCSL's (2003) work on learning-centred leadership (see Box 11.2) and on coaching (2005, and see Box 11.3), both of which present a consistent picture of the development of institutional culture

---

Box 11.2 Distributed and learning-centred leadership

Distributed leadership

Distributed and learning-centred leadership: two sides of the same coin?

In order to thoroughly explore what learning-centred leadership looks like in practice, one needs first to understand distributed leadership.

Leadership is a function that needs to be distributed throughout the organisational community. Yet educational institutions do not simply need lots of leaders working individually.

Distributed leadership means that there should be:

- lots of leaders, at all levels
- lots of action and learning-centred leaders.

It also needs to be:

- developed
- co-ordinated
- team-based.

Distributed leadership does not happen by accident, it has to be designed. It requires leaders and managers to let go of some of their responsibilities. It also requires them to mentor and coach the emerging leaders.

There is an interdependence between the two which means it is only when leadership is shared, is it truly learning-centred.

NCSL is exploring distributed leadership. Find out more about this work at: www.ncsl.org.uk/distributedleadership.

Box 11.3 Mentoring and coaching strategies

NCSL (2005) describe a structured programme of coaching:

Coaching [is] designed to have a positive impact at the organisational level through focused work with the individual client. The ... programme has three distinct phases:

> *Fact gathering* includes in-depth interviews and a battery of psychological tests. Colleagues and significant individuals in the client's personal life (nominated by the client) are also individually interviewed.
>
> *Planning and consolidation* begins with a two-to-three day 'insight session' during which the information gathered is presented to the client as a portrait which pinpoints strengths and shortfalls. This information becomes the basis for a development plan, which details specific and measurable goals and action steps.
>
> *Implementation* begins with the client enlisting the help of the employing organisation in providing resources and support for achieving specific goals. The consultants or 'coaches' facilitate the development process and interview selected individuals at intervals in order to check and re-tune the client's goals.
>
> The formal coaching relationship tends to continue for approximately two years, and ends when the client has developed a support mechanism for ongoing growth, which may include a coaching relationship with a sponsor or a more senior manager.

(*Source:* www.ncsl.org.uk/mentoringandcoaching)

---

in order to maximise alignment between the espoused values of the student learning experience and the management practices of educational leaders.

Leading and managing the project

The team of four colleagues which had been at the Edinburgh Change Academy was already implementing its own change project (on developing an institution-wide approach to blended learning using a Blackboard-based e-learning platform), made a natural steering group for the project, and supported the Fellowship holder in appointing the project officer – the boldly-named Organisational Learning Champion. This was a nine-month, fractional appointment which was made internally – the group felt that the limited timescale made it essential to work with a colleague who already knew the institution.

The person who was offered the position of Organisational Learning Champion was a known entrepreneurial figure who matched the desired profile for a change agent – a highly-skilled networker with clear understanding and experience of facilitating processes of visioning and action planning which could inspire others.

In practice, the steering group retained a 'hands-off' approach, and the Fellowship holder was left with a high degree of autonomy in terms of the detail of project implementation.

There were three broad phases to the project as planned:

1   an *information-gathering phase*, involving desk-based research and first-hand visits to businesses and institutions which professed a live interest in organisational learning;
2   a *design phase*, in which the systems of supporting professional dialogue were devised (including coaching, action learning and an internal Change Academy event); and
3   a *dissemination phase*, which was still ongoing several months after the end of project funding.

In practice, a fourth phase emerged which might be termed a *sustainability phase*, in which the project's work (and the role of the Organisational Learning Champion) metamorphosed into multi-stranded activity which was seen as an organic manifestation of the wider culture change initiative which the project seemed to have become in the eyes of its intended beneficiaries. The unpredictable nature of this phase chimes with Saunders's assertions on the complexity of change in higher education, applied within what he terms 'mutually adaptive systems' (2005: 23).

In addition to direct project funding, the LFHE also provided an Associate who performed a coaching role to several projects and thus facilitated potential networking between different institutions. Given that one of the project's stated aims was to introduce coaching into the College's systems, it was particularly fascinating to experience a model for coaching as a means of support for change projects.

The greatest strength of the Associate used by the LFHE was his skill in not over-emphasising the coaching process. He simply demonstrated it by example, in a subtle and understated way which was initially disarming. The coach acted as a sounding-board for the Fellowship-holder's attempts to make sense of the cultural change which was unfolding unpredictably around the project. Direct involvement in this process provided added conviction to the notion in the project's design that coaching should be one of the support mechanisms to be made available to project participants.

Crucial factors for success

- Recognition at national level gave internal credibility to the project, and a 'license to innovate' which was liberating and empowering.
- The available time from the supporting postholder, the Organisational Learning Champion, allowed for the strategic vision of the Fellowship-holder to be implemented.
- Learning from elsewhere was practicable because of the funding provided, and would have been difficult to achieve otherwise: visits to other higher education institutions, businesses, CEL, NCSL, innovation labs in the business and education sectors.
- Learning with others: the locally-based food company, Ginsters, participated in the internal Change Academy and provided invaluable new perspectives. The company also used the two-day residential experience to devise successfully an internal communications strategy.
- Funding for the internal Change Academy, which would not otherwise have been possible to support from institutional funds.
- The longer-term sustainability which was achieved through spin-off income-generating work. This focuses on workforce development in the newly-formed childrens' services sector, and on the creation of a College Innovations Lab. Neither was an originally-anticipated outcome, underlining the need for flexibility in determining the complex impacts of the change process.
- Tangible achievements in terms of quantifiable elements. From January 2005 (when four academic staff were engaged in knowledge transfer work) to October 2005, a total of 19 staff had become involved (15 per cent of academic community), and additional income was being generated by some of the academic units in the institution.
- The high visibility which the project had in the institution, supported by discussion at the College Management Team, and regular internal dissemination through the fortnightly newsletter for business and community reach-out activity, *interact*.
- New ways of bringing people together to develop and share new ideas – these were quite distinct from the more formal meetings which were the cultural norm elsewhere in the College.

Building on this last point, the processes of support which were facilitated by the Organisational Learning Champion and the Fellowship-holder turned out to be crucial, especially when these furthered the development of professional dialogue. These included the modelling (on an ongoing basis throughout the academic year) of coaching, mentoring and action learning, although not always labelled so explicitly. In one academic School, a voluntary action learning set met over a period of five months, at the instigation of the Fellowship-holder. This was the focus of a separate action research project, with the expectation of disseminating its findings more widely within the institution, and thus contributing to the cultural change process.

The internal Change Academy event was promoted internally shortly before the summer vacation of 2005, and attracted applications from five teams, each comprising between two and seven members. Teams were invited to make proposals for change projects they could start to develop over the two-day residential experience, held half an hour away from the College. Examples were given for the sort of projects which might be suitable, including those focusing on quality improvement, learning and teaching innovations, or generating income – covering a wider range than was suggested by the initial focus of the project on business and community reach-out. In practice, the four internal teams came up with diverse proposals covering curriculum development (Youth and Community; Geography), conference planning (Public Relations) and devising outdoor training for management development (Outdoor Adventure Education/Management).

The event was universally acclaimed by participants, who clearly felt that they had contributed to the creation of a unique experience. It was talked of several months later by some of the 22 participants – who represented almost 20 per cent of the academic staff of the institution – and two of the six academic schools in the College commissioned the Organisational Learning Champion to facilitate their own one-day Change Academy events during the same academic year.

Interestingly, several participants in the internal Change Academy spoke over the following months of their ongoing interest in what they called 'the change project', assuming that they felt there was an explicit strategic process underway even after the cessation of project funding. This appeared to be an example of change embedding itself in the culture of the institution and thus an indicator of successful project impact.

Barriers to innovation

While there was strong peer support for the project from other middle managers in the institution, and considerable interest from the academic community, the project remained somewhat peripheral to the key concerns of the College Management Team. This was probably due to the need to spend considerable time during 2005 on the two greatest priorities for the institution – of securing taught degree-awarding powers, and preparing for the introduction of top-up fees.

At times, resistance was drawn out from some senior managers when the Fellowship-holder and Organisational Learning Champion modelled innovation processes during management team meetings. There was an element of 'suspension of disbelief' when furniture was reorganised in order to enhance groupwork, but at the end of an hour of idea-generation, the room reverted to formal meeting mode. The impact of the project on the working practices of the Management Team as a whole has therefore yet to be felt. Indeed, there is some evidence that the *content* under discussion during the modelling was negatively affected by interference from the process.

This may, however, not be a lasting state of affairs, and the creation of the permanent Innovation Lab space may well contribute to change in the longer term.

One further potential barrier to sustained change may lie in the lack of continued funding for project activity, although clearly this was anticipated at the design stage. The management of regional business and community activity, under the auspices of funding from the Higher Education Innovation Fund, will enable the continuation of many aspects of the project's work in supporting new approaches to professional discourse across the institution, and outwards into the many partnerships in which its staff engage.

Recommendations

For any institution considering introducing cultural change which is intended to impact on the practices of professional discourse in an institution (or part of an institution), the experience of this project suggests that it may be worth taking into account:

- the role and credibility of the proposed change agents;
- the intended outcomes in terms of the behaviour and practice of the beneficiaries;
- the ways in which the project is branded internally (and possibly externally) – the use of the LFHE, HEA and Change Academy brands were all helpful to the learning organisations project;
- the proposed means of disseminating the project's work within the institution – a two-sided printed newsletter was highly popular in developing the project, and in driving demand for other forms of printed internal communication across the College;
- the need to build in flexibility in terms of the unpredictability of outcomes;
- the need for longer-term sustainability by embedding the change in mainstream institutional processes.

From a researcher's perspective, a number of issues are raised which would be worthy of further investigation. These include the need for longitudinal studies of the impact on professional behaviours and practices of using coaching, action learning and creative problem-solving techniques to drive cultural change in higher education institutions. A further need is raised by Senge which does not yet seem to have been investigated in the field of higher education management: to develop 'theory of what happens when teams learn (as opposed to individuals in teams learning)' (1990: 238).

Given the increasing certainty of unpredictable change in all aspects of higher education over the coming decades, it could be argued that no university or college can afford not to be driven by the values and practices of a learning organisation – they are at the core of the sustainability the sector so desperately needs to embrace.

References

Garrett, R. (2001) *The Learning Organisation*, Harper Collins: London.

Hannan, A. and Silver, H. (2000) *Innovating in Higher Education: Teaching, Learning and Institutional Cultures*, Society for Research into Higher Education/Open University Press: Buckingham.

Leadership Foundation for Higher Education (LFHE) (2005) *The Evolving Agenda*, Leadership Foundation for Higher Education: London.

McCaffery, P. (2004) *The Higher Education Manager's Handbook*, RoutledgeFalmer: London.

McGill, I. and Brockbank, R. (2004) *The Action Learning Handbook*, Kogan Page: London.

National College for School Leadership (NCSL) (2003) *Learning-Centred Leadership*, National College for School Leadership: Nottingham.

National College for School Leadership (NCSL) (2005) *Leading Coaching in Schools*, National College for School Leadership: Nottingham

Pedler, M. (1996) *Action Learning for Managers*, Lemos and Crane: London.

Ramsden, P. (1998) *Learning to Lead in Higher Education*, Routledge: London.

Revans, R. (1983) *ABC of Action Learning*, Chartwell-Bratt: Bromley.

Rowley, J. (1998) 'Creating a learning organisation in higher education', *Industrial and Commercial Training*, 30(1): 16–19.

Saunders, M. (2005) 'How can evaluation help manage complex change?' *Academy Exchange*, 2: 22–3.

Senge, P. (1990) *The Fifth Discipline*, Doubleday: London.

Sheffield Hallam University (2003) *Organisational Learning and the Future of Higher Education*, Sheffield Hallam University: Sheffield.

Trowler, P., Saunders, M. and Knight, P. (2003) *Change Thinking, Change Practices*, LTSN Generic Centre: York.

Chapter 12

Embedding equality and diversity in the university

Teresa Rees and Hannah Young

Developing good equality and diversity policies is relatively straightforward, but embedding them in the culture and arrangement of an organisation, so that they make a difference to people's lives, is quite a different matter. It was this challenge that the Leadership Foundation project at Cardiff University aimed to tackle. We sought to explore and develop strategies to enable the University to promote equality and diversity within all its policies, processes and 'ways of doing things'. We drew upon both public sector 'mainstreaming' approaches to promoting equality and private sector human resource management approaches of 'managing diversity'.

Mainstreaming involves the use of a range of tools to promote equality, and therefore equity, in all institutional functions and practices as well as in the working culture (Rees 2005). Managing diversity entails the development of strategies and the fostering of a work culture in which differences between people are valued on the basis that they can have commercial benefits (see Kandola and Fullerton 1998, ch. 4). Such benefits can include developing a diverse workforce to enhance creativity and innovation in research and development and widening recruitment pools to address skill shortages (Rübsamen -Waigmann *et al.* 2003). The project also drew on change-management theory to maximise the potential for achieving genuinely embedded and sustainable cultural and structural change.

This chapter describes the methods used to interrogate the institutional culture and identify replicable elements of good practice in promoting equality and diversity, both within the institution and more widely. It also outlines the way in which the findings then influenced current and future plans to embed equality and diversity within the institution.

Context

In 2004, Cardiff University merged with the University of Wales College of Medicine to become the ninth largest university in the UK. The vision of the new Cardiff University is to be world-class: its strategic plan is directed towards 'achieving the highest standards in research, learning and teaching in a rich and varied research-led environment where all staff and students can achieve their full potential'. In setting this goal, Cardiff shares with other higher education institutions (HEIs) the challenge of recruiting and retaining high quality academic staff and students from a wide international base – a context in which the development of fair processes and an inclusive culture assume increasing importance. Metcalf *et al.* (2005) identify equitable practices, such as fairness in pay and progression systems, as likely to enhance the capacity of universities to attract the best staff. Similarly, there is some evidence that an active recognition of diversity and effective management (rather than a mere presence of diversity within the workforce) reduces recruitment costs and improves retention of talented workers (Kandola and Fullerton 1998, CIPD 2005).

All HEIs are operating in the context of a rapidly evolving equality law and policy framework: they will soon be required to demonstrate that they are actively promoting equality in relation to sex and disability as well as race. Regulations now recognise discrimination on grounds of sexual orientation, religion or other belief and age. The new statutory Commission for Equality and Human Rights will enhance the potential for discrimination associated with these factors to be identified and challenged. While past progress in integrating equality within the Higher Education (HE) sector has been regarded as 'largely unmonitored and often fragmented', policy and funding frameworks now encourage a more proactive approach, at least in relation to race, disability and gender (Deem *et al.* 2005: 10).

The legal and political context for Welsh HEIs is further enhanced by the provisions of the *Government of Wales Act 1998*. This obliges the National Assembly for Wales to pay 'due regard' to equality of opportunity '*for all*' (our emphasis) in all that it does. The duty has been interpreted as requiring that equality is defined broadly, rather than being restricted to specific strands and that it should be taken into account in all areas of activity (Chaney 2002). The Assembly has developed a proactive approach to mainstreaming and has provided a lead in the public sector in Wales, for example on developing strategy and capacity building (National Assembly for Wales 2004). This provides a positive context for Cardiff University and the promotion of equality envisaged through this project.

The process of restructuring and policy review prompted by the merger and by the National Framework Agreement on pay and conditions provided an opportunity for Cardiff University to place greater emphasis on the active promotion of equality and to move towards the mainstreaming approach adopted by the Welsh Assembly. The Pro-Vice-Chancellor for Staff and Students (and the Leadership Foundation Fellow on this project) is an expert adviser on mainstreaming to the European Commission and the Assembly: she led on this project with the newly-appointed University Equality and Diversity Manager.

Planning

The aim of the Cardiff project was to develop mechanisms to integrate equality and diversity across University structures and systems and to build capacity in the institution to ensure that this integration was sustained. This represented a shift from simply addressing direct discrimination to tackling indirect discrimination through promoting equality. Key objectives were to:

- gather baseline data to enable the measurement of the University's progress in embedding equality and diversity within its culture and functions;
- identify and describe replicable elements of existing good equality practice; and
- develop a range of practical strategy options for embedding, and building capacity to deliver equality and diversity across the institution.

The process of developing the motivation, knowledge and skills to integrate equality proactively across the institution would necessarily represent a cultural shift and some operational changes for University staff. The focus of the project plan was to gather evidence from a range of internal and external sources which would equip the institution's leaders with tools to manage the change process. This meant identifying relevant information to motivate change, developing practical suggestions to guide the process of how to change and understanding best practice to develop a vision for change (based on the Lewin's three stages of change, explained and adapted by Schein 1999; Fowler 2005).

In the planning stage, steps were taken to develop the infrastructure needed to support the process of promoting and embedding equality. A revamped University Equality and Diversity Committee, chaired by the Pro-Vice-Chancellor for Staff and Students and attended by the Vice-Chancellor was established in October 2004. This developed a new equality and diversity policy, which reflected a broader interpretation of equality than that required by legislation and which emphasised the importance of *promoting* equality within the institutional culture. An Equality and Diversity Support Team, comprised of Deputy Directors of each of the University's administrative directorates, was established to drive forward the work of the committee across the University's administration. Before merger, neither institution had employed a specialist equality or diversity practitioner. In each, as in many HEIs, responsibility for equality had been located in the Human Resources function. In 2004, an Equality and Diversity Manager post was created and placed instead within the Corporate Services Directorate, reflecting the pan-institutional remit.[1]

A range of methods was used to meet the key objectives of the project. The University has a devolved structure comprising 28 academic Schools and six administrative Directorates. As a first step, all the Heads of the Schools and Directorates were surveyed via an online questionnaire to determine arrangements for promoting equality and managing diversity at this second-tier level. Academic Schools produce strategic plans on a bi-annual cycle: these were analysed for evidence of the integration of equality and diversity. The University's general strategic plan with accompanying supporting plans (relating to learning and teaching, widening access, and so forth), and administrative development plans were also scrutinised for their treatment of equality and diversity. The results of the survey and document analysis provided a baseline understanding of institutional awareness and progress towards embedding on which to base the development of equality and diversity strategies.

The document surveys revealed some examples of good practice in promoting equality and diversity, which were used to develop case-studies to be shared more widely across the University (see Box 12.1).

Supplementary interviews were conducted with individuals involved in good practice, whether because of their specific job role (such as working in widening access, staff development, community development or disability support) or being a trade union representative or because of their specific interest and skills in this area. Those mentioned specifically by Heads of Schools or Directorates within the surveys were often able to suggest others who had not yet been identified in this way, who were also contacted and interviewed for information about their work and their perception of its value to the institution.

The project also used auditing and benchmarking surveys to inform understanding of the extent to which current cultures and structures are able to promote a positive working environment in which equality and diversity are valued. These included Opportunity Now and Race for Opportunity benchmarking surveys and a series of focus groups and interviews facilitated for the University by the Work Foundation.

Methods used to identify replicable examples of good practice external to the institution included a review of HEI websites; a literature survey of equality and diversity within HE; and a literature and web survey of other organisations promoting themselves as valuing diversity through the development of codes of conduct based on dignity and respect. Campus unions provided further examples of good practice. The Fellow and project officer also gathered information from attendance at a range of conferences and meetings.[2]

The project was based partly on action-research principles, and as such allowed for regular reflection on what was discovered about the culture and working of the organisation and reviews of the ways in which equality and diversity could be embedded most effectively in light of that understanding. This aspect of the project has perhaps been the most important. A greater understanding of organisational working has led to closer working with

---

Box 12.1 Examples of 'good practice' in promoting diversity and
equality

Case study 1: Equality action-planning by the School of City and Regional Planning

Since 1999, the School of City and Regional Planning has had a 'promoting equal opportunities' policy, code of good practice and action
plan, which is monitored by an equal opportunities committee. These
documents are written in a manner which explains their relevance to the
work of the School and gives practical applications such as 'in planning
everyday activities such as venues for social events we need to be sensitive to the diversity of our students – not everyone is, or wants to be,
comfortable in a pub, for example'. Equal opportunities appears on the
School's web homepage and further information about activity, such as
their survey of student experience, is included via weblinks.
                         (See http://www.cardiff.ac.uk/cplan/school/eq-opps.html)

Case Study 2: Working in partnership to promote good relations through an academic research centre

In the run-up to the opening of a new research centre – the Centre
for the Study of Islam in the UK – the School for Religious and
Theological Studies employed a community development worker and
ran a series of community engagement events, taking the University's
mobile exhibition unit to Mosques in Cardiff. The Centre's partnership
with the local community is maintained though the Centre's Advisory
Group which includes members of the South Wales' Muslim Community and the Welsh Assembly Government Equality Policy Unit. The
Centre specialises in the social scientific study of Islam and Muslims in
contemporary Britain and has been described as 'an accessible, vibrant
and inclusive hub of learning about Islam in Britain for Muslims and
non-Muslims alike'.
      (See http://www.cardiff.ac.uk/schoolsanddivisions/academicschools/
                                relig/research/centres/islam-uk/index.html)

---

individual Directors and Heads of Schools to integrate equality and diversity
within existing development plans and according to existing priorities. Linking equality and diversity to a wider 'positive working environment' agenda
has led to greater buy-in and a better understanding of the joined-up,
embedding approach.

Leading and managing the project

The project drew together the equality expertise of the Fellow and project manager with a substantive understanding of the wide range of organisational functions, culture and key structures, together with an acknowledgement of the potential for resistance to change. The University strategic plan describes the organisational structure as 'devolved and flexible'. Focus groups indicated some of the opportunities and challenges arising from this structure. Interpretations ranged from 'expanding, dynamic, forward-looking and flexible' to a sense that it was difficult to determine a 'University culture' as there were significant differences among departments, described as 'mini-institutions'. When asked to suggest improvements, participants identified a need for greater communication, harmonisation and leadership. The survey of Heads of academic Schools and administrative Directorates painted a similar picture. In response to being asked to identify priorities for embedding equality and diversity more effectively in the University, a range of Schools and Directorates highlighted the need for a unified strategic approach across the University, communication of clear guidance, training and awareness-raising, and integration through the committee structure.

One of the challenges of the project was to provide leadership and guidance which created a vision broad enough to form a sense of organisational direction and unity, but with sufficient practical relevance to engage individual Schools and Directorates. Analysis of the online survey and of Strategic plans demonstrated limited understanding of the way in which equality and diversity were likely to be relevant within the University environment. In common with Deem *et al.*'s (2005) findings in the sector more widely, Schools were most likely to identify equality and diversity as being relevant to provision for disabled students or widening participation activities. An ongoing theme of the project has therefore been the need to provide practical relevant examples and to explain how these link to overarching ideas of recognising difference, being explicit about processes and the importance of participation within decision-making.

One of the clearest examples of a structural recognition of the importance of embedding equality has been in the University Registry where a new post has been created. The person in this role works with Schools to extend the University's accessible curriculum project, but also has the support of the Registry senior management team to identify priorities for impact assessment and to increase awareness of the relevance and application of equality and diversity across the directorate. Some academic Schools have begun to engender a clearer team responsibility among members of their School equality and diversity committee. From these, a contacts network is beginning to evolve, with a groundswell of enthusiasm and desire for more cross-University working. So far, arrangements appear most successful where more than one individual in the School or Directorate plays an active role in the promotion of equality and diversity.

Enthusiasm was also generated through the establishment of different forms of networking. The University's women professors were brought together at a dinner hosted by the Leadership Foundation Fellow. Members of a Sexual Orientation Working Group, convened to develop a sexual orientation policy and implementation plan, made the case for a virtual network for lesbian, gay, bi-sexual and transgender (LGBT) staff. Through the project, the views of these groups and those of trade union representatives have been sought and acted upon. Information about the action taken has been fed back so as to encourage further participation and engender broader cultural change.

The project has aimed to integrate the activities of a range of University projects under the banner of *developing a positive working environment*. Making explicit connections between the work to promote equality, dignity at work, the national pay framework, stress management, Investors in People, improving accessibility of the University estate and improving IT access is beginning to break down the sense of a lack of uniform strategy captured in the focus group comments above. In the words of one colleague, 'things have made a lot more sense since you've been involved', and of a University Council member 'it's great to see how these things all fit together'. The latter emphasises the extent to which this integration is helping to create a vision to motivate the adoption of equality within working culture.

It was recognised that equality and diversity aims should be aligned with long-term strategic aims in order to be embedded effectively within the institutional structure (see Friday and Friday 2003). The Equality and Diversity Committee provided a substantial response to the University's review of its strategic plan. The Leadership Foundation Fellow and Equality and Diversity Manager delivered presentations to University Council and University Board and addressed a meeting of Heads of Schools when strategic plans were being developed to suggest mechanisms by which equality and diversity could be integrated within planning processes. Practical examples of how this might be done were provided, using the internal and external case-studies identified through the project. Examples provided to the Board included the work of Shell (see Box 12.2), BT Group (see Box 12.3) and Astra Zeneca, which demonstrated the importance of communicating explicitly a commitment to equality and diversity through practical understanding of its application.

Guidance to Schools was focused around developing the infrastructure to support the long-term embedding of equality and diversity. This included ensuring that there is a transparent governance structure, making clear commitments to developing a culture based on dignity and respect, and analysing management information to identify the specific equalities issues relevant within the School. This general guidance was complemented with support to Schools through the attendance of the Equality and Diversity Manager at

Box 12.2 Shell

Shell's global diversity and inclusiveness standard, together with an implementation framework and 'roadmap' provides the organisation-level business case as well as practical information about the range of functions in which diversity needs to be applied and the methods for achieving change. See www.shell.com (then click on 'how we work' and 'making it happen'). In the UK, Shell communicates this commitment by providing '102 items of evidence for recruiting, retaining and developing women' as part of its profile on the 'Where Women Want to Work' website: http://www.www2wk.com.

Box 12.3 BT plc

BT promotes a practical understanding of what is meant by their commitment to diversity and inclusivity by their participation in a range of partnership activities (including, for example, projects relating to dignity at work, pregnancy discrimination and supplier diversity). The company has supported the development of nine employee networks – comprising groups of staff who are, for example, disabled, Muslim, from an ethnic minority, or lesbian, gay, bisexual or transgendered. The company has also provided a good practice model for understanding different staff needs and including a diverse range of views within organisational decision-making.
(See www.btplc.com/Societyandenvironment/
SocialandEnvironmentReport/section.aspx?sectionId=D84F4962-
053D-4722-B1B8-9A1C4324BCE5)

School equality committees and providing information and other resources to support the development of School equality action plans. This type of activity and dialogue between equality practitioner and functional expert replicated the successful approach taken within the University's accessible curriculum project.

What helped

Undoubtedly, the support and leadership provided by the Vice-Chancellor was highly significant in ensuring that the equality agenda was taken seriously. Both the literature on mainstreaming and managing diversity demonstrates the importance of leadership and commitment from the top. Having a PVC with a high equality profile and a dedicated Equality and Diversity Manager helped to consolidate the significance of the equality agenda.

Although at the start of the project the University already had an Equality and Diversity Policy, the evidence of our surveys suggested that there was not a clear understanding of the types of behaviour that would promote or frustrate an inclusive University culture. A University Dignity at Work and Study Policy was developed to make explicit the over-arching aspiration to develop a positive work and study environment and to explain the responsibilities of all staff in promoting that culture. The policy drew on examples from organisations that have moved away from bullying and harassment policies to codes of conduct promoting mutual respect, for example Motorola (see Box 12.4), BAE systems (see Box 12.5), and King's Lynn and Wisbech NHS Trust (see Box 12.6). The policy has been widely welcomed by Heads of School and the University and there are plans to develop a promotional strategy at the beginning of the next academic year.

Box 12.4 Motorola's Code of Business Conduct

This code has been in place since the 1970s. It outlines the key beliefs that guide business activity and are expected to be demonstrated by employees. These are described as follows:

Uncompromising integrity means staying true to what we believe. We adhere to honesty, fairness and doing the right thing without compromise, even when circumstances make it difficult.

Constant respect for people means we treat everyone with dignity, as we would like to be treated ourselves. Constant respect applies to every individual we interact with around the world.

(See www.motorola.com/content/0,,75-107,00.html)

Box 12.5 BAE Systems' 'Respect at Work'

BAE Systems, as part of their Corporate Responsibility Programme, have a 'Respect at Work' policy. The emphasis on promoting respect, rather than simply eliminating bullying and harassment, emphasises a positive vision in which all employees have a stake: 'We want a working environment where everyone feels valued and respected and can contribute to the success of BAE systems.'

(See www.baesystems.com/corporateresponsibility/
workplace/respect.htm)

Box 12.6 King's Lynn and Wisbech NHS Trust 'managing mutual respect'

In 2005, King's Lynn and Wisbech NHS achieved the gold standard kitemark in its implementation of the Department of Health 'Improving Working Lives' Standard. One of the initiatives used was a review of the Trust's harassment and bullying policy to change its emphasis to 'managing mutual respect'. See further 'Strategy: Best Practice', *People Management*, 30 June 2005.

At an early stage of the project, the University made links with a range of organisations able to offer information, advice, practical resources and opportunities to share good practice. The Fellow already had strong links with Athena (Women in Science, Engineering and Technology), the Wales Equality Reference Group (representing a wide range of equality dimensions) and Chwarae Teg (promoting women's education, training and employment in Wales) and the University was already a member of Opportunity Now and the EOC Equality Exchange. During the course of the project, the University became the first member of Stonewall's 'Diversity Champions Cymru' (Wales), joined 'Race for Opportunity' and established links with 'JIVE' (the joint interventions network to improve the position of women in Science, Engineering and Technology). The Equality and Diversity Manager already had links with the Equality Challenge Unit and became a member of the Welsh Liaison Group. Developing these partnerships with a range of organisations has enabled the University quickly to improve levels of equality competence, display direct recognition of different groups within its community and raise the profile of its progress in embedding equality and diversity. In recent months the University has hosted the first Stonewall 'Diversity Champions Cymru' seminar and the Equal Opportunities Commission consultation on the gender equality duty Code of Practice.

The merger created the opportunity for particularly close working with Cardiff and Vale NHS Trust to work towards embedding equality not only within but across organisational structures, an approach which is supported by the Welsh Assembly Government's *Making the Connections* strategy (Welsh Assembly Government 2004). The Trust and the University have reciprocal arrangements for representation on their Equality Steering Group and Equality and Diversity Committee respectively and have recently joined with local councils and health boards to conduct a joint consultation on access to health and social care.

External regulatory influences, such as the need to develop an Equality Code of Practice for the RAE, and the prospect of an emphasis on equality within Institutional Review have undoubtedly been helpful in reinforcing the key message of the project – that equality should be integrated within institutional policy, practice and culture. In addition, results of the National Student Survey and International Student Barometer increased internal awareness of equality issues, for example on the need for prayer rooms. While the timing of these was coincidental, they appeared to carry greater weight amongst many than arguments based on compliance with changes in the law.

What hindered

A key factor that has been associated with successful cultural change is the availability of statistical data (Smith 2003). The process of merging two large institutions and moving to new systems for holding staff and student data created difficulties in obtaining good management information. Such information is a key tool of managing diversity, since it can provide evidence for example, that the strategy has measurable cost savings in relation to recruitment. At a deeper level, disaggregated monitoring data is a key tool of equality work, providing evidence of the patterns of inequality which are consistently found to exist (for example in recruitment, progression, pay and complaints procedures) for those who might otherwise be sceptical of the presence of institutional barriers. The relative lack of accessible statistical information within the institution limited the reach of the project, as it became much more difficult to make a sound business case to support the promotion of equality and diversity and align equality to strategic aims. This is now being addressed.

The project aims are broad. Working across a wide range of areas, it became more difficult to manage increasing requests for advice, support and guidance which were the inevitable result of heightening awareness. Mechanisms planned to manage this difficulty and to maintain the development of equality competence across the institution include the establishment of an equality and diversity website, a more formalised contact structure and a series of secondments to work with the Equality and Diversity Manager. However, the time taken to develop the materials needed to support these activities has in itself hampered progress.

Results

Mainstreaming equality is a long-term agenda. This project has focused on ensuring that institutional prerequisites, such as awareness-raising, capacity-building, management information systems, disaggregated data and suitable policies and institutional support are developed. Significant progress has been made. We have achieved greater understanding of the organisational structure and culture(s) of the institution. We have mapped good practice and grown the capacity to promote equality within the institution. We have developed a resource base of information and good practice, as well as robust partnerships to inform a best practice approach, generating interest and enthusiasm from individuals. We have started training on impact assessment, which is encouraging reflection, but this needs further support.

Lewin and Schein's change theories (Schein 1999) are based on the idea that once people are motivated to change, it is possible to introduce to them a new perspective, then to 'refreeze', to integrate the new perspective into their behaviour. One of the challenges of mainstreaming equality is that we are asking people not simply to see another perspective, but to develop the skill of continuously challenging their own perspective. It has been helpful through the course of the project to explain equality and diversity (as does Shaw 2004: 13) not as a 'thing' or 'concept' but as a process. It is not doing more but doing things differently. However, this characterisation demands from people a consistent motivation both to the process of change and to their own learning. It is not sufficient to overcome resistance to change. 'Tell me what to do and I will do it', as was said to us during the course of this project, will not result in a regular and consistent evaluation of the effects of inequality. Potentially, it makes mainstreaming equality more difficult to introduce than other forms of structural and cultural change. A way of addressing this difficulty may be to look more widely at the culture of learning, development and reflection in the institution and at Cardiff, close links are being made between equality and diversity work, training and development, stress management and Investors in People. It is interesting to note that the Directorates beginning to engage most actively with the implications of embedding equality and diversity are those concerned with staff development and University learning and teaching.

There is a huge breadth of relevant academic expertise within the institution which could be used more effectively in embedding equality and diversity across the institution. University staff and students have a wide range of opportunities to develop their own understanding through access to public events and library resources. During the course of the project the University recruited Professor Carole Pateman, an internationally renowned feminist political theorist and hosted lectures by Professor Lynne Segal, a leading gender studies expert and Ben Summerskill, Chief Executive of Stonewall. The School of Social Sciences hosted one of a series of ESRC-funded seminars on mainsteaming equality (designed to bring together policy-makers, academics and activists). The School also runs a part-time MSc in Equality and Diversity which equips its students (all working in the equality field) with the skills required to advise on embedding equality and diversity within organisations.

Recommendations

Embedding equality and diversity entails a mind shift in ways of thinking and working. Our experience suggest that there are merits in capitalising on existing good practice, learning how the institution works, building on enthusiasm and expertise, developing networks and making links with other agendas. Prerequisites for success include leadership from the top and expertise. However, we have been assisted by drivers such as the developing legislative framework and the RAE code of practice.

We have learnt the important practical lesson of being pragmatic and seizing opportunities as they arise – by working with people when they are interested and enthusiastic. At the same time, there is a need for persistence in chasing through change even when it has been agreed. It is important to sustain a 'lobbying' role. It is helpful to give clear examples of progress and publicise these widely; probably not enough time has been spent so far on publicity and the development of promotional resources. As with all equality work, it is essential not to lose your temper or become irritating, and always to maintain a sense of humour!

Overview and where to next?

Our intention is to continue this work on culture change through developing links with other agendas and growing expertise and confidence through the institution. By seeking to integrate equality into the strategic planning process and linking it into the broader positive work environment thinking, hopefully more policies and processes will seek to promote equality. A website is planned that will document work and provide resources and links. Membership of equality organisations will inform and assist our work, for example we have recently joined Athena which will lead to some initiatives on women in science, engineering and technology. Mentoring schemes are being expanded to more categories of staff. Staff networks are being set up. Awareness-raising and briefing sessions as well as more training courses are being developed and delivered on a range of equality issues.

Cultural and organisational change is a long-term and challenging agenda. The Leadership Foundation project gave us a head start in enabling us to focus on developing a strategic approach to this agenda, one which is beginning to show some results already. There is inevitably much more to be done.

Notes

1 While it was originally planned that the Equality and Diversity Manager would work in tandem with a project officer to deliver the project aims, it only proved possible to recruit to one of these posts.
2 The project was also the focus of an action learning exercise undertaken by the Fellow on a Leadership Foundation for Higher Education Top Management

Programme: it therefore benefited from advice, experience and support from the TMP tutor and action learning set participants.

References

Chaney, P. (2002) ' "An Absolute Duty": the Assembly's statutory equality of opportunity imperative – the Standing Committee on Equality of Opportunity, in J. Barry Jones and J. Osmond (eds) *Building a Civic Culture: Policy, Process and Institutional Change in the National Assembly*, Volume II, 2001–02, Institute of Welsh Affairs (IWA): Cardiff, pp. 225–43.

Deem, R., Morley, L. and Tlili, A. (2005) *Negotiating Equity in Higher Education Institutions, Equal Opportunities and Diversity for Staff in Higher Education Project 3*, Report to HEFCE, SHEFC, HEFCW available at: http://www.hefce.ac.uk/pubs/rdreports/2005/rd10_05/.

Fowler, K. (2005) *Managing Change: A Guide for those Working in Higher Education*, Association of University Administrators (AUA): Manchester.

Friday, E. and Friday, S. (2003) 'Managing diversity using a strategic planned change approach', *Journal of Management Development*, 22: 863–80.

Kandola, R. and Fullerton, J. (1998) *Diversity in Action: Managing the Mosaic*, 2nd edn, Chartered Institute of Personnel and Development (CIPD): London.

Metcalf, H., Rolfe, H., Stevens, P. and Weale, M. (2005) *Recruitment and Retention of Academic Staff in Higher Education*, Research Brief No. RB658, Department for Education and Skills: London.

National Assembly for Wales (2004) *Report on Mainstreaming Equality in the Work of the National Assembly*. National Assembly for Wales Equality of Opportunity Committee: Cardiff.

Rees, T. (2005) 'Reflections on the uneven development of gender mainstreaming in Europe', *International Journal of Feminist Politics*, 7(4): 555–74.

Rübsamen-Waigmann, H., Sohlberg, R., Rees, T., *et al.* (2003) *Women in Industrial Research: A Wake-Up Call for European Industry*, Office for Official Publications of the European Communities: Luxembourg, and at http://europa.eu.int/comm/research/wir.

Schein, E. H. (1999) 'Kurt Lewin's Change Theory in the field and in the classroom: notes towards a model of managed learning', *Society for Organizational Learning Journal*, 1: 59–74.

Shaw, J. (2004) 'Mainstreaming equality in European law and policymaking', *European Network Against Racism*, available at: www.enar-eu.org/en/publication/mainstreaming_04_en.pdf.

Smith, M. E. (2003) 'Changing an organisation's culture: correlates of success and failure', *Leadership and Organization Development Journal*, 24: 249–61.

Tatli, A., Ozbilgin, M., Woman, D. and Mulholland, G. (2006) Change agenda: managing diversity, measuring success. Chartered Institute for Personnel and Development: London. Available at: http://www.cipd.co.uk/NR/rdonlyres/809E744B-5018-4592-9544-ADC2A311937F/0/mandiversca0306.pdf.

Welsh Assembly Government (2004) *Making the Connections: Delivering Better Services for Wales*, http://www.wales.gov.uk/themesmakingconnection/content/mtc-document-e.pdf.

Chapter 13

Developing and embedding global perspectives across the university

Chris Shiel

The project addresses directly, sustainable development and global perspectives and is enabling Bournemouth University to progress the sustainability agenda by developing awareness of the complexity of these issues (through staff development and a range of new activities). An inclusive approach to change is resulting in a plan of action that will secure the commitment and participation of staff and students. Approaches that seek to embed these issues across the students' experience are important, indeed necessary, if we are to produce graduates who are equipped to face the contradictions and uncertainties of this increasingly globalised world.

Professor Paul Curran, Vice Chancellor,
Bournemouth University, 2005

Context

As the 'Decade of Education for Sustainable Development' (UNESCO 2005–15) gets underway and with the emphasis placed by UK government on global citizenship and sustainability, the project described in this chapter seems particularly timely. The chapter presents an initiative at Bournemouth University (BU), to achieve a step-change in institutional commitment to the development of global perspectives and global citizens (who understand the need for sustainable development).

The Leadership Foundation Fellowship Programme (LFFP) award in 2005 enabled research to be undertaken, to develop a strategy and action plan with the aim, that by 2010, all graduates of BU will be aware of and confident in dealing with issues relating to equity, justice, diversity and sustainable development. The Fellowship provided an opportunity to build upon the foundations of work initiated, to embed global perspectives and sustainable development across curricula.

Background to global perspectives

BU has been developing 'global perspectives' (GP) since 1999, when a group of staff volunteers came together with a colleague from Development Education in Dorset (a local non-governmental organisation) to discuss how GP might be developed and how graduates might be equipped to be responsible global citizens, in a context where diversity and complexity are increasingly apparent. The group formulated a 'Global Vision for BU' which was endorsed by Senate in 2000. Subsequently the work of the group became formalised within the institutional committee structures, reporting directly to the Learning and Teaching Committee. The group was expanded to include broader representation (see Box 13.1) and the status of the group was elevated significantly when the PVC (Academic) became the Chair.

The aims of the GP group are to encourage global awareness amongst staff and students and to promote the development of:

- curricula that acknowledge the importance of global perspectives and sustainable development;
- opportunities for students and staff to develop knowledge skills and

---

Box 13.1 Composition of the global perspectives (GP) group

Pro-Vice Chancellor Academic (chair)
Head of Programmes, Institute of Business and Law
Education Manager, Development Education in East Dorset
President of Students' Union
Students' Union Member
Student Representatives
Head of Learning and Teaching, Services Management
Associate Head of Academic Services
Head of International Programmes
University Chaplain
Head of Bournemouth Media School (BMS)
BMS Senior Lecturer
Design, Engineering and Computing Academic Senior Lecturer
Head of Marketing, International and Corporate Relations
Head of Learning and Teaching, Institute of Business and Law
International Office, International Student Support Manager
Institute of Health and Community Studies, Senior Lecturer
Head of International and Corporate Relations
Conservation Sciences, Senior Lecturer

understanding to allow them to make an effective contribution to a global society;

- a culture where diversity is respected and individuals feel empowered to bring about change;
- an enhanced understanding of the concept of 'citizenship' and what this means, both in the local community and at an international level.

Although substantial progress had been made at BU, a more strategic thrust was seen as necessary to secure a step-change in institutional commitment.

Planning

The project planning stage highlighted the importance of developing a persuasive and compelling rationale for change, coupled with a consultation process that would facilitate maximum 'buy-in' from staff and a tangible 'output', in the form of a strategy document and action plan. A benchmark of achievements to date was required and an analysis of the 'push' and 'pull' factors (drivers for change), such as the political, economic, environmental, employability contexts. A 'SWOT' analysis and language that would enable a business case to be put forward would support the change agenda and address criticism that these issues are too much about 'ideology' and constitute a 'political agenda'.

The planning stage mapped out the data collection process, identified the need to include the perspectives of 'stakeholders' – particularly students, staff and employers – and provided a framework for development and target dates.

It would have been easy (and simpler) to have adopted an approach that involved largely desk-based research, resulting in a strategy document, but influencing stakeholders was seen as critical to implementation. The data gathering process was thus seen as serving a dual function: collecting information while at the same time engaging in a variety of conversations to educate, communicate and raise ideas in a way that was non-threatening. The outcomes of these conversations and the ideas that surfaced would feed directly into an action plan.

In the early stages of planning it was decided that rather than focus solely on curricula, the action plan had to cover all aspects of the University business: it was felt inappropriate to advocate one thing for students, if the University did not 'walk the talk' with regard to sustainable development. The plan was thus broadened to encompass issues relating to estates, finance, purchasing, etc. A schedule of meetings was drawn up to include consultation with the range of stakeholders.

In preparation for these meetings a number of early papers and presentations were put together to articulate terminology. These early 'summaries of the concepts' served as a starting point for discussion. They were sometimes tailored to particular audiences, sometimes emphasised links with other strategies (or 'hot' issues) and became enhanced and developed as the schedule of meetings progressed. One example included highlighting the link to the diversity agenda (Box 13.2) and explaining the implications of the approach for teaching and learning.

Box 13.2 What is the link to diversity?

The global citizen values cultural diversity and will be able to manage sensitively across cultures. The global perspectives agenda has developed at BU to support the ethos that:

> We live in one world. What we do affects others and what others do affects us, as never before. To recognise that we are all members of a world community and that we all have responsibilities to each other is not romantic rhetoric, but modern economic and social reality.
>
> (DfES 2004: 5)

The global citizen is someone who:

- is aware of the wider world and has a sense of their own role as a world citizen
- respects and values diversity
- has an understanding of how the world works economically, politically, socially, culturally, technologically and environmentally
- challenges social injustice
- participates in and contributes to the community at a range of levels from the local to the global
- is willing to act to make the world a more equitable and sustainable place
- takes responsibility for their actions.

(Oxfam 1997)

It is suggested that examining a subject or issue through a global perspective is essentially about taking a broader approach to that subject that:

- values methodologies, techniques and academic analysis from other cultures
- challenges and discards prejudice
- considers with sensitivity the effect of our actions on others locally and globally, both now and in the future
- questions Eurocentric, rich-world, restricted perspectives and takes into account viewpoints and circumstances from all regions of the world
- presents learners with the capacity to calculate the risks of decision-making

- acknowledges the global forces that affect us all and promotes justice and equality
- empowers learners to bring about change
- provides an international curriculum and seeks opportunitites to develop students' international awareness and competence.

Developing such specific examples provided an opportunity to persuade different audiences that the project aligned with their interests. They also served to ascertain whether individuals, or particular groups, had concerns with language and terminology. In most instances these examples triggered conversations which then resulted in positive suggestions and new ideas; in some instances the language used was changed and developed to reflect the most widely accepted terms.

Leading and managing the project: an inclusive approach to change

The nature of the project called for 'participative evolution' (Dunphy and Stace 1993) involving a collaborative, consultative process. An organisational development (OD) approach to change was adopted in the belief that 'the primary motivator for how change is accomplished resides with the people in the organisation' (Benjamin and Mabey 1993: 181). A further factor in selecting the approach was that a focus on 'process' aligned well with the academic background, experience and value system of the change facilitator and is more appropriate in a context where the goals are unclear and the concepts are ambiguous.

The work of Quinn (1980) provided a useful 'organising framework' that was loosely and philosophically adopted. Different activities are undertaken in what might seem like a three-stage approach (although these are not intended to be neatly sequential):

- create awareness and commitment incrementally
- solidify progress incrementally
- integrate processes and interests.

In practical terms this involved:

- meetings, presentations, conversations and more meetings with stakeholders;
- surveys of staff and students (to understand the starting point of the learner), focus groups and a series of development workshops;
- desk-based research to develop the 'persuasive rationale for change', and the 'trigger layer' (Buchanan and McCalman 1989) by examining

environmental opportunities and threats, including the policy context, business case and other key agendas;

- populating an action plan and developing strategy during the process of change;
- implementing small changes during the process;
- sharing, refining and amending the action plan, as data emerged and improvements were suggested.

The variety and order of meetings and presentations that took place is presented in Table 13.1. Some of these events were formal presentations, others were one to one conversations.

The early meetings were largely about 'need sensing' (in the sense used by Quinn) through conversations with stakeholders. These served a multiple purpose: 'amplifying understanding' (of the concepts and strategy and considering alternatives), collecting data and 'building credibility' (laying the way for future strategy). 'Legitimising viewpoints' meant that sometimes things would surface that were negative and often surprising (in terms of what they revealed about individual's world views (e.g. 'I think the solution is imperialism') but with experience, these were often quickly countered with logic and

Table 13.1 Dissemination and data gathering

Activity led by Fellow	Parallel activity led by Project Assistant
Heads of School (6)	International Office
Head of Marketing and Corporate Communication	Chaplaincy
Centre for Research and Knowledge Transfer	Students' Union
School Executive Groups (6)	Head of Purchasing
Professional Services Exec.	Environmental Strategy GP
Equality and Diversity Officer	Purchasing Team
Head of Estates	SU Volunteering Office
Sport and Recreation	Desk-based research ongoing
Student/staff workshop	Staff survey
Academic Development and Quality	Student Focus Groups
PVCs (Academic, Finance)	Student survey
Director of Human Resources	Student workshops (4)
Partnerships, Access and Community	Equality and Diversity Officer
Staff development in three Schools	
Two University wide staff development workshops	
Presentation to show link to employability at BU Employability conference	
Major conference: 'Education for Sustainable Development: Graduates as Global Citizens'	
Presentation to Learning and Teaching Development Committee	
Presentation to Senior Management Team	
Completed Report and Action Plan to Senate	

persuasion. 'Building political support' was critical to ensure momentum and a number of informal meetings were useful to establish alliances, create pockets of commitment and implement smaller changes that would eventually contribute to the whole.

While meetings with senior stakeholders were in progress the Project Assistant undertook two focus groups with students to gather their views on global perspectives. This was followed up by a survey of a wider group of students. An electronic staff survey was also undertaken to find out more about the perceptions of a broader group of staff, to gather ideas as to how global perspectives could be introduced more widely and to identify inhibitors to change.

What helped

Critical to the success of the project was the appointment of two Project Assistants, who in the early stages 'job-shared' the role. Their backgrounds (one in international development with experience of research but also in campaigning, the other with an environmental background, excellent administrative skills and a passionate activist for change) provided considerable synergy, enabled excellent teamwork and brought a sense of excitement to the work.

The approach to change worked well and secured greater commitment than could have been imagined, enabling the widest possible contribution to policy development. The process of sometimes relentless meetings and conversations ensured that by the time the strategy document was produced and went to the Senior Management Team (SMT), there was very little in its content that was a surprise and nothing that was opposed. SMT suggested a few more items for the Action Plan and the report passed on through Senate, with full endorsement.

Visible 'outputs' along the way (e.g. a bi-annual publication; launch of Global Cinema; introducing Fair Trade, etc.) and high-profile activities, including an international conference, increased awareness of activities. These in turn created a snowball effect widening stakeholder engagement with the issues.

Ensuring that the project work was aligned to parallel developments being championed by others (for example, 'enhancing employability' (Shiel *et al.* 2005) and 'internationalisation') strengthened the push for change. Such alignment resulted in GP work being incorporated into a broader set of activities, where others developed the GP perspective within their own project plans and agendas.

Collecting data directly from students and staff provided a useful 'reality check' on achievements, surfacing their concerns and allowing for the identification of areas for future development. Comments from students such as: 'Bournemouth is international because of the numbers of overseas students –

pity I never got to talk to any of them' (UK student) and; 'the tutor asked us to get into groups. I looked around and everyone had groups. I felt bad but then realised that three other Asian students were also left standing. We had to work together because UK students do not want us in their group', serve as harsh reminders that things should change.

Similarly staff comments such as 'Well they [international students] come here to do a UK degree so why should we adapt what we do?' and 'I teach students to shaft the competition – it's incompatible with caring about diversity' revealed the challenge of changing perspectives and the need for staff development.

The process of widening out one-to-one interviews with staff continued to reveal new insights. For example, an interview with the Diversity Officer about his experience raised several interesting points about student perceptions of diversity and led to immediate changes. His experience confirmed that there is a tendency for UK students to avoid events that include the words 'global', 'international', or 'diversity' because they do not think that these terms apply to them. The Diversity Officer's recommendations were:

• To think carefully about how we phrase events or news when communicating with students.
• To try to change attitudes through raising awareness and working with the student societies more, to encourage inclusion and mixing of international and UK students.

Continuing to develop and refine ways to show what is meant by a 'global perspective' and articulating the links between GP, sustainable development and internationalisation, solidified understanding of what were sometimes perceived as 'vague concepts' and 'not related to my agenda'. A number of models and diagrams were used along the way, to explain to staff that these are not separate and therefore competing agendas. Continuing to develop and refine diagrams and text contributed to broader understanding and support. Figure 13.1 represents a model that evolved to enhance understanding of what is meant by a global perspective and the factors that contribute to global citizenship.

This was accompanied by sets of text to support further understanding of the link between GP and the component parts, as illustrated in Box 13.3.

Resources booklets were also developed to 'educate' and explain Fair Trade and Globalisation. Ensuring that the former were located at all catering outlets provided visible symbols of the institution's commitment to change.

What hindered

There was very little that hindered taking this initiative forward, apart from the time it took to mobilise resources initially. Quinn (1980) highlights the

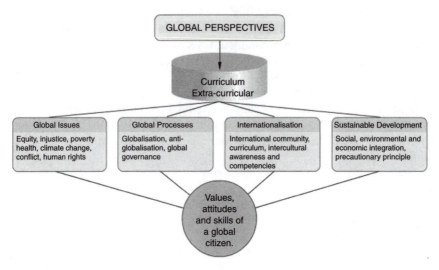

Figure 13.1 Aspects that contribute to the development of global citizens in a higher education setting.

Source: Shiel and Mann 2006

Box 13.3 Example of set text used to show relationship between SD and GP

The relationship between sustainable development and a global perspective

A global perspective emphasises 'human values' but not at the expense of ignoring the need for sustainable development and environmental issues. An understanding of sustainable development is part of the knowledge required of the global citizen who will also comprehend the potential impact of local activity on the global, and vice versa, with regard to such things as pollution and climate change, exploiting natural resources, etc. Adopting a global perspective requires that actions that secure more sustainable development are pursued; actions that are not sustainable are challenged and change is sought to ensure that development does not compromise the quality of life for future generations.

(Extract from BU document)

importance of 'buffers' and the need to build in 'slack'. The project timeframe was tight and was eventually extended, to provide the slack to capitalise on new opportunities, including the arrival of a new Vice-Chancellor.

In the early stages some staff found it difficult to get to grips with the concepts but developing explanations and resources to educate helped overcome this.

Results

The final outcome of the project was a strategic report and action plan for change: *A Global Perspective at Bournemouth University: Education for Global Citizens and Sustainable Development*. The report presents an analysis of the compelling drivers for change in terms of the external environment, policy context and the links to the employability agenda and includes a summary of activity being undertaken by other institutions across the sector.

The report culminates in a series of recommendations for governance, finance, leadership, estates, energy, waste, purchasing, staff, curriculum and pedagogy, extra curricula and research, organised around three categories:

- corporate responsibility and behaviour – the University as a global citizen;
- curricula and pedagogy – embedding GP into curricula;
- extra-curricular activities to support citizenship and international awareness.

The action plan identifies approximately 80 actions, areas of responsibility and timeframes. Table 13.2 provides a sample of just a few.

'Small wins' along the way

The advantage of Quinn's approach to change, is that by the time 'strategies begin to crystallise, pieces of them were already being implemented' (1980: 86). This brought a sense of excitement to the project and reduced some of the anxiety that might have been caused by such a huge action plan.

'Deliverables' before the strategy and action plan passed through Senate included:
- curriculum change;
- launch of a bi-annual publication the 'BUGLE' (Bournemouth University Global Local Education);
- launch of the 'Global Cinema';
- links to the 'employability' strategy with GP being audited as part of Annual Reports on Programme Monitoring;
- GP included as part of the Personal Development and Planning website;
- a major conference on Education for Sustainable Development: Graduates as Global Citizens;

Table 13.2 Action plan (extract)

Theme: category	Aim	Action
Institutional level: waste	Promote waste minimisation both within the university and with suppliers Extend recycling initiatives to recycle additional items	Communications campaign to raise awareness Broaden focus to include initiatives for students based on existing recycling initiatives focused on staff
Fair-trade	Achieve 'fair-trade' status	Set up steering group; formulate policy; develop agenda with Students' Union and plan education programme; submit application
Curriculum level: internationalising	Enhance the international experience of all students Ensure that pedagogy is appropriate to diversity of learners and encourage 'active' approaches to learning that empower learners	Develop international opportunities for industrial placements in other countries and provide a 'one-stop shop' approach Develop pedagogic approaches that enable students to learn from international students (walk in my shoes/storytelling) Staff development to share activities such as Bafabafa and development education approaches

- the development of a Fair-trade University;
- a staff development programme and the provision of resource material to facilitate the inclusion of global perspectives in learning and teaching;
- collaboration with the International Office and closer alignment with 'internationalisation' strategy;
- developments with the Students' Union to extend community activities and the development of the GP website.

Learning from the survey of students and staff

The data obtained from the student focus groups and the student survey (answered by 268 students) informed the action plan but triggered a range of workshop initiatives and suggestions for curriculum change, implemented during the course of the project.

The data collected from students highlighted:

- *Defining terms*: generally students did not know the meaning of terminology that relates to basic global issues. This included the meaning of sustainable development (most thought the term meant continuous economic growth); fair-trade; the WTO and the G8.

- *Students' main concerns*: the environment, poverty, equality, terrorism were listed as the main concerns of students (irrespective of nationality).
- *How international/global is BU?*: students generally considered that BU is international 'because of the number of international students'. Discussion suggested however, that there is limited integration with home students and international students felt that activities targeted at international students reinforced a sense of separateness and created 'ghettos'. (Evidence of this sense of isolation, was indicated by speakers at the UKCOSA Conference 2005.)
- *GP in the curriculum*: overall students suggested that there was not enough coverage in their curriculum and supported the idea of a separate GP unit. They felt that GP could be integrated into the curriculum better if staff had more expertise in the relevant fields, such as sustainable development. Tutors could support learning more effectively if they ensured that group work encouraged diversity. Proactive management of group formation might break down barriers to integration. Case studies from other countries would also be useful, as well as compulsory studies in global issues and cultural awareness studies.
- *Extra-curricular activities*: students suggested that more events should be organised to encourage home and international students to mix whilst avoiding words such as diversity, global or international. 'Home' students feel that such events are exclusively for international students and do not attend. Students are keen to engage in 'volunteering' and 'fundraising'; courses however, do not often incorporate these learning experiences.

The 59 staff who responded to the staff survey revealed that while some good work had already been achieved, many staff did not fully appreciate the importance of the 'international dimension', or the extent to which an international curriculum and experience including cross-cultural learning might enrich the learning process. A summary of the data collected through the staff survey showed:

- the inclusion of global processes (social, economic, political and environmental) in course content is quite high although there is scope for further inclusion; coverage of global cultures and case studies could be improved; opportunities for students to volunteer and engage with the community are low.
- Levels of undergraduate and postgraduate understanding of global, cultural and ethical issues are generally not as high as one might expect. Students are more likely to appreciate 'multiple perspectives and interpretations', be aware of 'cultural assumptions and biases' and 'ethical issues': they are less likely to understand 'global issues', 'international trade' or 'reflect on global perspectives issues in relation to their own lives'.

- Most staff see the relevance of global perspectives to their subject areas (81 per cent) and 63 per cent think students will understand the relevance, only 7 per cent of staff suggested that the curriculum was too crowded to cope and/or the requirements of professional bodies made change impossible.
- Approximately one third of respondents indicated that there is a 'lack of staff expertise and 'awareness'; only 20 per cent indicated a 'lack of academic interest' and 20 per cent a 'lack of institutional drive'. A similar proportion of staff were unsure how to respond.
- In terms of international influence/activities such as international field trips, exchange programmes and language learning, the results found that these influences were low in both undergraduate and postgraduate programmes and staff generally perceived international activities as being of 'low importance'.
- Regarding the main challenges to introducing GP, encouragingly, a large proportion (47 per cent) responded that there are no challenges; time (12 per cent) and funding (9 per cent) are seen as important by some staff.
- The majority of staff are interested in staff development or are already engaging with GP, or consider it as a possibility; only 20 per cent are not interested.
- Twenty-five per cent of staff are already broadening their subjects to include global perspectives. Others suggested that the introduction of case studies, more time, conference opportunities and extra funding would help.
- Views towards introducing GP as a 'separate unit' or as part of existing units were varied. There was an almost equal divide between those that favour the idea of a separate unit to those that favoured integration into units.
- The top three responses to how the University could do more to develop GP identified: through teaching, providing staff development and providing resources.

The lack of importance that staff placed on international influences, international experience and activities such as international exchange and opportunities for language learning was the most disturbing feature of the results. 'Internationalising' staff will be one aspect of the developing HR strategy in the future. Staff development workshops will be provided to show that learning should harness the opportunities that diversity and 'multicultural interaction provide' (De Vita and Case 2003) and to develop 'cross-cultural' awareness in the belief that 'only systematic development of staff's cross-cultural skills will enable them to bring out the potential of students' contributions in the classroom and facilitate them working together as members of multi-national work groups' (Black 2005: 15). Developing assessment strategies that require the students to learn from other cultural viewpoints will contribute to breaking down the 'ghettos' to which the data collected from students referred.

Fortunately, staff were generally very positive about engaging with activities to broaden the curriculum, provided that they are supported through workshops and resources.

Recommendations

> We need to look at sustainable development as a whole – how to use our resources without wasting them; how to teach and learn about sustainable development; how to generate the skills, knowledge and understanding to allow us to fulfil our duty as global citizens.
>
> (Rt Hon Charles Clarke, Sustainable Development Action Plan for Education and Skills)

The work undertaken for this project addressed directly, concerns raised by policy makers that education must address sustainable development and prepare students for a global society. Some institutions have undertaken some excellent work on the environmental side of sustainability (HEPS 2004; Copernicus members); some have developed the global perspectives agenda, with less attention to sustainability in an environmental sense and others have focused considerably on 'internationalisation'. Very few universities have sought to address the agenda in an integrative and holistic way. The main recommendation from this project is that institutions should seek to embed global perspectives and sustainable development throughout curricula, while at the same time addressing sustainable development in the way that the institutional business is discharged.

If we do not promote change then we are responsible for delivering an education that supports the maintenance of the status quo. In the words of Boyer (1994):

> In the end, educating for a global community has to do with attitude – the attitude that we relate to one another. That attitude amongst graduates will produce a more literate and thoughtful population. This will not occur, however, through special courses, but rather by changing the way academics think about their work.

Further recommendations relate to the process of change.

The nature of the project involved dealing with ambiguous concepts and the need to win 'hearts and minds' in the context of unclear outcomes. The approach to change was successful and is thus, recommended, with the caution that it is time-consuming and requires considerable energy and enthusiasm on the part of the change champion.

The approach involves 'implementing' at the same time as 'formulating' strategy: implementing actions along the way is recommended ('small wins' contribute to momentum).

Sometimes the most challenging people to persuade can turn into the most powerful allies. On the other hand those who 'buy in' to an idea too easily have not always fully understood and can be 'off-message' later. Do not be put off by 'difficult' people or dismiss their potential.

Ensuring alignment and integration with other strategies is critical if a project such as this is to succeed and not become a 'fad' that evaporates with time.

Where to next?

BU is implementing the actions that arose from the project and this will continue over the next five years, achieving 'Fairtrade' status for example, was an action that was achieved in June 2006.

A new Vice-Chancellor has inspired a shift in institutional direction, the development of a new corporate plan and further institutional change. As new institutional strategies emerge, and the staff base changes, it will be important to ensure that support for the development of global perspectives continues and is reflected in new strategy documents. As BU develops to become a 'world-class' university, it will be important to ensure that an essential aspect of a world-class reputation, is the development of graduates who are empowered to contribute to a better world.

Concomitant with developing a 'world-class' university, will be extending 'global reach'. This will enhance bringing the 'global into the local' and will serve to enrich the international experience of UK students and staff. In parallel, consideration will be given to strategies for 'internationalisation at home' (Shiel 2006) and to the development of more inclusive learning, teaching and assessment practices, appropriate to multi-cultural learners as well as securing greater participation of UK students in local and global initiatives.

Research to contribute to the theoretical foundations of the concepts will be ongoing: funded doctoral research will explore the contribution of development education approaches in a higher education context. Funding has also been secured from the Department for International Development (DfID), for a 'Skills for Life' project that will involve working with development education in Dorset. The project will extend opportunities to create and share learning practice to build development education capacity within higher education, to enable staff and students to develop the skills to participate effectively in decision-making in their local and global community and to become agents of change. It is hoped that with time, BU will become a 'hub' of a variety of community networks to extend sustainable development and the notion of global citizenship.

References

Benjamin, G. and Mabey, C. (1993) 'Facilitating radical change: a case of organization transformation', in C. Mabey and B. Mayon-White (eds) *Managing Change* (2nd edn), Paul Chapman Publishing: London.

Black, K. (2005) 'A review of factors which contribute to the internationalisation of a programme of study', *Journal of Hospitality Leisure, Sport and Tourism Education*, 3(1).

Boyer, Ernest L. (1994) Keynote speech at 'Building the Global Community: the next step', at the American Council of International Intercultural Education (ACIIE), and the Stanley Foundation Conference, November, http://www.stanley foundation.org/reports/CCI.pdf.

BU Global Perspectives Network (1999) *A Global Vision for Bournemouth University*, June, internal publication.

Curran, P. (2005) 'Preface' to *A Global Perspective at Bournemouth University: Education for Global Citizens and Sustainable Development*, internal publication.

De Vita, G. and Case, P. (2003) 'Rethinking the internationalisation agenda in UK Higher Education', *Journal of Further and Higher Education*, 27: 4.

Department for Education and Skills (DfES) (2004) 'Putting the world into world-class education: an international strategy for education and skills', www.dfes.gov.uk.

DfES (2005) 'Learning for the future: the DfES Sustainable Development Action Plan 2005/06' http://www.dfes.gov.uk/aboutus/sd/docs/SDAP%202006%20FINAL.pdf.

Dunphey, D. and Stace, D. (1993) 'The strategic management of corporate change', *Human Relations*, 46(8): 905–20.

Higher Education Partnership for Sustainability (HEPS) (2004) HEPS Report 'On course for sustainability', Forum for the Future, www.forumforthefuture.org.uk/docs/publications/237/On%20course%20for%.

Mann, S., Shiel, C. and Williams, A. (2005) 'Global perspectives at Bournemouth University: views from students and staff', Bournemouth University Conference, *Education for Sustainable Development: Graduates as Global Citizens*.

Oxfam (1997) *A Curriculum of Global Citizenship*, http://www.oxfam.org.uk/cool-plantet/teachers/globciti/.

Quinn, J. B. (1980) 'Managing strategic change', *Sloan Management Review*, 21(4): 67–86.

Shiel, C. (2006) 'Cultural diversity: are we doing enough?' BMAF Subject Centre Conference, *Managing Diversity in Teaching and Learning*, Oxford.

Shiel, C. and Mann, S. (2006) 'Becoming a global citizen', *Bournemouth University Global Local Education (BUGLE)*, internal news publication.

Shiel, C., Williams, A. and Mann, S. (2005) 'Global perspectives and sustainable development in the curriculum: enhanced employability, more thoughtful society?', Proceedings of the Bournemouth University Learning and Teaching Conference, *Enhancing Graduate Employability: The roles of learning, teaching, research and knowledge transfer*.

Chapter 14

The challenge of strategic leadership

Leading cultural change

Gwen Wileman

Introduction

The UK university sector is facing a huge strategic HR agenda. This chapter examines how a university HR Directorate can refocus its structure and way of working to become a genuine business partner at every level of the university's business. Driving change through people as the university's critical asset is essential to success in an increasingly turbulent HE sector.

Three aspects are key to the transformation of HR:

1   The introduction of an HR Service Centre which seeks to maximise the use of technology yet maintains a very strong customer focus.
2   HR managers and advisers who are aligned with Faculty and Directorate management teams and operate as genuine business partners at both corporate and faculty level.
3   The design and implementation of a meaningful measurement process for people management activity which is integrated with the performance management processes of the university.

The De Montfort University context

De Montfort University (DMU) is a large, vibrant and ambitious university whose vision and strategic objectives are summarised in Box 14.1.

In broad terms it has 20,000 students, 3,000 staff and a turnover of £115 million per annum.

The University takes the effective leadership and management of people very seriously and the strategic objectives of the University have significant people implications. The University is committed to the recruitment and retention of excellent employees whose personal aspirations are aligned with the University's strategic objectives. There is a clear recognition at the highest level in the University that the people the University is employing are critical to its success. This is a real commitment rather than rhetoric as the improving staff survey trends indicate that DMU if not yet a great place to work for

---

Box 14.1 DMU: key strategic objectives

1 Develop and promote a distinctive academic portfolio
2 Enhance quality
3 Optimise student profile
4 Strengthen research and regional engagement
5 Maintain financial sustainability
6 Maintain and develop the quality of our staff
7 Maintain and develop supporting infrastructure and the environment.

---

everyone is clearly moving from being a good place to work for most to becoming an even better place to work for almost all.

DMU recognises that the continuing and significant efforts of the current staff are the major contributor to success as a University and thus seeks to further enhance its reputation as an employer of choice both locally and nationally in the sector.

The HR transformation project, led by the LFFP Fellow and the focus of this chapter, aimed to refocus and develop the HR Directorate to meet the increasing demands placed upon it in the light of these aspirations.

Rationale for change

Much of the HR literature and forward thinking HR practice is based on the work of David Ulrich and his work on business partnership in organisations. This provided a useful model to assess ways in which the university could drive people strategy alongside the business strategy in a way which creates synergy and success. The Ulrich model works effectively in some organisations and sectors and has begun to generate some sound research. The case study material which was a useful basis to think through the best approach for a university environment and the research conducted by Michael Syriett (2004) for Business Intelligence – *Redefining Strategic HR* is particularly relevant (see Boxes 14.2 and 14.3).

Prior to 2004 DMU already had a well-developed and effective model of HR advisers attached to faculties and working with the Faculty and Directorate executives on their people management agendas. This, however, needed further development to operate more pro-actively and the underpinning HR services and information activities needed to be separated out to provide focus for significant technical and service development. The policy work needed further integration. The challenge for the HR Leadership Team was significant as those individuals, too, needed to refocus their roles to become strategic business partners as well as senior service managers.

Box 14.2 HR: a strategic role

The findings of the Business Intelligence's research among 200 HR Directors and senior managers show that HR departments most likely to take on a strategic role in the organisation have the following three characteristics:

• a conviction at board level that HR has a key role to play in supporting the achievement of business goals
• the capability within HR to understand and contribute to the shaping and delivery of business strategy
• the ability to demonstrate that HR is making a measurable contribution to business success.

Redefining Strategic HR
Business Intelligence
2004

Box 14.3 Critical success factors that contribute to strategic success

The research findings identified six Critical Success Factors for HR:

• ensure efficient service delivery
• speak the language of business
• demonstrate the business benefits of HR
• create processes and practices for partnership
• develop business skills within HR
• build HR's credibility as a business partner.

Redefining Strategic HR
Business Intelligence
2004

Equally important is the change in perspective required by management colleagues. Many HR functions, despite significant efforts of very talented professionals, are seen to be reactive to and adaptive to changes in business strategy. This can create an organisational- and people-based 'lag' – a delay that often frustrates the leadership and senior managers in the organisation and can lead to a tendency to react with rapid deployment of initiatives, programmes and events which may have limited long-term sustainable impact. The concept of a partnership at both corporate and faculty level to tackle the people management agenda requires, and continues to require, high-level relationship-building skills, and financial and business skills as well as exemplary professional HR capability.

Research indicated that in those businesses where employee 'discretionary contribution' is at the highest level the role of HR had subtly but significantly changed. DMU wanted to really understand the drivers of employee engagement which could deliver the highest level of discretionary contribution at DMU.

Informed by this research the senior team at DMU took on board the need to formulate and drive a people agenda – led by the Director of HR but overtly sponsored and supported by the Vice-Chancellor and other members of the senior executive team.

In response to this the Director of HR challenged her own Directorate structure and adjusted its core proposition to the business towards improving and increasing levels of service and enhancing reputation through 'added value' activity and contribution.

The HR Directorate could point to many significant contributions to the people management aspects of the ambitious organisational change agenda pursued by the University over the previous four to five years. However, the current and anticipated speed of change and evolution within the university sector now suggested a real and urgent need for the HR Directorate to prepare for a further step change in its effectiveness. This required the refocus of the internal structures of HR and redefinition of stakeholder relationships with the rest of the University to enable HR to be a genuine business partner across every part of the University's business.

Aims and objectives of LFFP fellowship project

The rationale for change was well understood. However, its impact on the HR function and its university stakeholders was wide ranging.

The Leadership Foundation Fellowship Project set out to support the transformation of HR in two specific ways:

- to clarify the role of an HR Business Partner in the University setting – and develop key members of the HR Team to undertake this role effectively;
- to improve the accessibility, analysis and practical use of HR information to support achievement of the University's strategic HR agenda and focus management on those 'vital few' employee performance indicators as levers for change.

The first of these two strands included a shared understanding of the role of the HR Business Partner in the DMU context, a change plan to embed the new role with management colleagues and a competency framework to identify areas of strength and development within the existing HR team.

The second strand of the project was to identify the key employee performance indicators which provide effective indicators of business success and the integration of the 'vital few' employee indicators with the University's performance management processes at corporate, faculty and individual level.

These two strands of the project to deliver HR Transformation was to some extent an artificial distinction as many other University-wide initiatives (e.g. a review of the University' strategic planning and performance monitoring process, the rewarding and recognition of our approach to teaching excellence and the negotiation of the National Framework Agreement with its underpinning role profiles, competency frameworks and reward strategy) needed to be fully integrated and in themselves are critical contributors to DMU's changing people agenda.

Broadly the project had a number of phases.

> *Phase 1* was a wide-ranging literature search and best practice review within the sector and outside it, and both nationally and internationally. Of particular relevance was a study tour to nine Australian university HR departments to gain perspectives on what constitutes 'best practice'.

> *Phase 2* was the work with HR team members, management colleagues and expert consultants to explore the application of best practice, tools and approaches which would best meet DMU requirements, and to commence the process of capacity building.

> *Phase 3* was implementation, and aspects of this are still ongoing and indeed subject to review of lessons learned from the early implementation and moving towards a culture of continuous improvement.

This was definitely *not* a linear project – but rather an approach to real culture change in people management approaches and capacity-building at DMU about which the university is continually learning.

Project approach: making it happen at De Montfort University

The HR Team at De Montfort University, before the commencement of this project, was considered to be forward thinking, professional and comprised of many talented individuals. This was both an advantage and disadvantage when embarking on the process of refocusing the team. The main advantage, of course, was that there was a very sound foundation on which to build an HR team who well understood the rationale for change at a professional level.

The disadvantages were twofold.

- First, natural feelings of uncertainty as roles, ways of working and Line Managers changed. This created a period of significant turnover and instability in the HR service team which had a detrimental effect on 'quality of service' and, therefore, a damaging effect on the reputation of HR across the University.
- Second, the impact of this, in the early stages, quite naturally led individuals to feel that not only was there personal uncertainty but also this was impacting, negatively, on their professional and personal pride in the service they provided.

Attempts to involve and communicate with the wider team were only partially successful in the early stage, and the process of implementation has taken longer than anticipated.

The 2005/06 academic year for HR at De Montfort University was an extremely challenging one, due to the implementation of two major new pay and grading structures (the National Framework and Senior Staff Pay and Grading Project), TUPE transfer of the Bedford Campus to create the University for Bedfordshire and management of a period of Industrial Action by Academic Staff over the 2006 national pay claim.

All of these were delivered successfully to timescale. However, the high workloads and significant challenges meant insufficient time was available for structured team development and individual personal development to support the transformation.

The development plans we were able to achieve, the inherent professionalism and experience of the team and the 'opportunistic' team working and 'partnership' opportunities created by the Directorate agenda last year enabled the putting in place of important building blocks for the next phase of transformation which is to commence in October 2006.

Human Resource advisors (HRAs) in Faculties

In terms of relationship building with management colleagues and understanding the core business, the location of HR advisors in Faculties for up to four days per week, and their full participation as members of Faculty Executive teams, has been successful, as confirmed by recent structured reviews with Deans.

Partnership working

For the HR leadership team – partnership working with both Trades Unions and senior management colleagues throughout the pay and grading negotiations and implementation (and its successful completion ahead of the national schedule) has created a real sense of strategic partnership with Deans and Directors across De Montfort University.

Business Partnership Forum

The Business Partnership Forum includes the senior leadership team, the HRAs and the HR Services Manager and provided a useful forum to involve the wider team in the strategic change process.

Early difficulties have been overcome by some very positive examples of team working, e.g. this group provided input to the HEFCE Self-Assessment Tool for people management, which meant that De Montfort University was one of only 17 HEIs to meet the requirements of evidence-based improvement in people management across seven dimensions. This resulted in consolidation of rewarding and developing staff and funding into DMU's core grant.

A new strategic plan

In developing the strategy and operational plans to support the new De Montfort University strategic plan, the leadership team have created both the processes and climate for cross-team working across the HR Directorate and it is believed that this will provide a further significant shift in DMU's capacity to respond to an increasingly challenging agenda.

Office refurbishment

The image and working environment of the HR Department has been transformed by the recent building work and office refurbishment which has created the positive image of a twenty-first century HR Department.

The impact on pride, culture and customer focus of the service team has been huge and has reinforced a strong culture of continuous improvement and service improvement, including the launch of Service Level Agreements with Faculties and Departments.

In summary, the change process was a difficult one for all involved, and whilst the process was not as 'structured' as originally planned, but instead has been an attempt to build capacity. Progress has been good and the impact of the HR contribution to De Montfort University is now recognised as increasingly significant, resulting in the enhancement of the reputation and strategic impact.

Results and key learning points

A refocused HR structure and way of working was implemented in September 2005. The key features of this transformation were to:

1   refocus expertise and resource on key University priorities with clarity of accountability for delivery;

2 create 'space' for senior HR team to deliver a more pro-active input to DMU's Strategic HR agenda;
3 Human Resource Advisors (HRAs) 'closer' to Faculties and Departments – both in location and by operating a pro-active 'business partner' model;
4 build on professional strengths of the relevant team and create a potential development route for team members;
5 better integration of HR policy development and practice;
6 integrated HR services with a focus on process and systems improvement.

A number of organisational development initiatives have supported the structure change. Examples include:

1 Role profiles were agreed with the team, although as new managers take up post these are being kept under continuous review.
2 A set of HR business partner competencies was developed and these were useful to identify early development needs. These now need simplification and refinement as the business partners develop their roles and a review of their effectiveness (see Table 14.1). Table 14.1 outlines the roles encompassed within the post of Director of Human Resources and this has been developed further to demonstrate how the *content* varies for different roles in the HR Team.

Table 14.1 HR business partner competencies (role profile: the roles encompassed within the post of Director of Human Resources are shown below)

Role	Context	Description
Designer	Setting direction	Thinking about programmes and services in fresh, exiting ways, learning from and responding to colleagues and clients
Designer	Organisational development	Knowing the institution and its success drivers; anticipating the impact of external changes on the institution; providing business leaders with organisational feedback
Designer	Developing strategy	Identifying and influencing key stakeholders; managing stakeholder expectations; ensuring the involvement of key stakeholders in the strategic process; using strategic models and tools to facilitate development of strategy
Constructor	Making links	Aligning HR initiatives and projects with Institutional/Departmental business requirements

Continued

Table 14.1 continued

Role	Context	Description
Constructor	Adding value	Creating new, useful measures and assesses HR's added value; identifying and taking opportunities for HR to make a difference; running own HR area as a business
Constructor	Originating action	Originating action to improve existing conditions and processes; using appropriate methods to identify opportunities, implement solutions and measure impact; using HR knowledge to achieve business objectives
Facilitator	Supporting change	Developing plans to turn strategy into action; maximising capability and readiness to achieve strategy
Facilitator	Supporting implementation	Provides managers with the knowledge, tools and techniques to implement change programmes
Facilitator	Managing relationships	Creating forums (formal and informal) and harnessing tools and techniques and specialist knowledge to enable managers to interact, discuss, problem solve; managing conflict situations effectively
Leader	Functional	Providing inspirational vision setting clear direction and performance standards and clearly defined role boundaries; empowering and delegating
Leader	Service performance	Motivating with involvement, praise and attention; giving people the power to make decisions
Leader	Service improvement	Running HR or team with HR as a business; providing HR with feedback from the business
Transferor	Sharing skills and knowledge	Encouraging and enabling people to learn and acquire new skills/knowledge
Transferor	Giving feedback	Coaching managers in behaviour change and understanding others
Censurer	Specialist technical knowledge know-how	Challenging business leaders to consider legal, compliance and good practice issues within the organisation; helping to resolve organisational dilemmas
Censurer	Championing values	Prompting business leaders to consider value issues within the organisation

3   The newly appointed HR Services Manager has now completed a plan for transformation of this service area and this has now commenced. Key features are efficient delivery every time, right people doing right work, maximum use of technology with a major focus on customer service.
4   Development plans for the team and individuals have been only partially completed due to the significant workload priorities this year and this is a critical part of the change plan to ensure continued progress.

The next DMU Strategic Plan – 'Preparing for 2010 and beyond' is now being launched. The continued and increasing contribution of the HR Directorate to support the University's plan is critical and continued development of the HR function is essential.

The HR Directorate adds value at four levels:

• lead development of corporate strategic HR agenda;
• lead on delivery of key strategic HR initiatives, plans and policies;
• provide ongoing proactive specialist HR advice to inform corporate strategy and plans and ensure consistent implementation in Faculties and Directorates;
• provide exemplary HR services, occupational, health and saftey services and professional development and training services.

Key employee indicators which underpin success

The old adage 'people are our most important asset' has been a stock phrase for many a company director and annual report. The research undertaken for the Chartered Institute of Personnel and Development (CIPD) 'Evaluating human capital' indicated that in many of organisations this phrase is little more than empty rhetoric and in reality many critical business decisions are made without any real understanding and knowledge of the value of people.

For DMU the need to really understand the value of our people as assets is an important, if difficult quest and the learning from the LFPP project has delivered only a partial solution to this 'holy grail'.

The current approach to 'people asset monitoring' at DMU has improved significantly over the last year or so. This includes access by managers to an on-line employee information service for their faculty/directorate, annual reports to the Board of Governors and a review of employee information as part of the University's internal performance management process. However, this is not yet embedded or accurate enough to provide well-used meaningful employee information and analysis which is sufficiently robust to engender the full confidence of the senior management team.

Box 14.4 CIPD: 'Evaluating human capital'

Produced as part of a five-year CIPD programme of work investigating the link between the way people are managed and business perform-ance, Professor Harry Scarborough (Warwick Business School) and Dr Juanita Elias (BRASS Research Centre, University of Cardiff) researched the ways in which ten major UK-based firms from a range of sectors evaluate their human capital. Their findings indicated that there is no single measure which can reflect adequately the richness of the employee contribution to corporate performance. They developed the concept of the virtuous human capital circle.

Their analysis suggests that measures are less important than the activity of measuring and that human capital cannot be the subject of a one-size-fits-all measurement tool but that it is possible for an organisa-tion to measure and manage human capital using methodology designed to suit their own needs and goods.

(CIPD: 'Evaluating human capital' 2002)

People asset monitoring

People asset monitoring is critical as it underpins the ability of the HR business partners to achieve credibility and demonstrate added value. A number of activities which supported the people metrics aspect of the HR Transformation project are continuing and are moving DMU in the right direction, but more needs to be done.

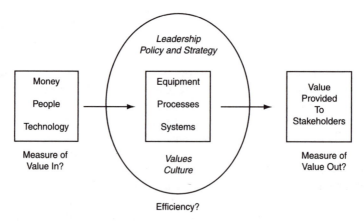

Figure 14.1 People as assets: the value chain.

Source: Mayo 2001

Examples include:

- staff survey data – available at faculty/directorate and corporate level including trend data;
- people targets incorporated into organisational monitoring process;
- pilot work in partnership with Professor Andrew Mayo on development of a people asset monitor in the Faculty of Health and Life Sciences (see Figure 14.1);
- input to strategic planning and monitoring process via people management framework;
- implementation of the people management self-assessment tool.

What helped and hindered delivery: a summary

A number of factors helped the project get off the ground in a positive and constructive manner, moving on to make real progress:

- input from HR team and management colleagues at DMU about what would work here;
- input from expert writers, consultants and practitioners;
- opportunity to reflect and explore best practice via conferences and international study tour to Australia;
- inspiration, focus and funding from Leadership Foundation Fellowship.

However, there were some factors which hindered progress with the change initiative:

- lack of dedicated project resource;
- destabilisation in HR team and high turnover of staff;
- urgent workload imperatives, e.g. National Framework implementation.

Nevertheless, real capacity-building has begun and a vision of where DMU would like to be in terms of partnerships in all faculties clarified. It remains to keep building on the success of this project and letting the present successes entice and breed further success.

Where next?

The 2006/10 Strategic Plan – 'Preparing for 2010 and beyond' is underpinned by a supporting HR Strategy based around nine key themes which need to be delivered to achieve the business goals:

- create a culture of pride and commitment
- structured organisational and leadership development

- performance management and reward framework
- recruitment and selection strategy
- high-quality professional development and training
- create a culture of health and safety and employee well-being
- HR planning process
- e-enabled HR processes
- HR policy review and development.

The HR Directorate Plan builds on the HR transformation activity so far and articulates how it will be led, organised and resourced to deliver DMU HR strategy in partnership with Faculty and Directorate colleagues.

Conclusion

This chapter outlined the steps taken at DMU to develop a twenty-first-century HR Directorate, highlighting significant progress. The revised structure and way of working within the HR Directorate are being embedded and now yielding results. The new HR strategy is more business focused and measurement is in place at corporate and Faculty/Directorate level.

The introduction of the HR Services model of delivery is demonstrating clear benefits but requires further development and a plan of process re-engineering is ongoing to realise its full potential. The Business Partner Model is developing well and needs to be further enhanced and supported through team development and better integration of HR services and training and development. Further strategies to influence some Deans and Directors of the real benefits of the partnership are still required.

The 'holy grail' of people metrics remains a challenge – as it does for many businesses, but progressing DMU's thinking on those metrics that really make a difference to business performance is now clearly well underway.

References

Chartered Institute of Personnel and Development (CIPD) (2002) 'Evaluating human capital', CIPD Bulletin (updated 1 Sept 2004), CIPD: London.
Chartered Institute of Personnel and Development (CIPD) (2004) 'Business partnering: a new direction for HR', CIPD Report, October, CIPD: London.
Elias, J. and Scarborough, H. (2004) 'Evaluating human capital: an exploratory study', Human Resource Management Journal, 14(4): 21–41.
Gratton, L. (2004) 'Means to an end', People Management, 10(17): 20.
Incomes Data Services (IDS) (2004) 'HR case study: The Royal Bank of Scotland Group', IDS HR Studies Update, 769: 14–17.
Mayo, A. J. (2001) The Human Value of the Enterprise, Nicholas Brealey Publishing: London.
Millar, M. (2004) 'Getting the measure of its people', Personnel Today, Dec: 6.

Syriett, M. (2004) 'Redefining Strategic HR. How to integrate HR with Corporate Strategy', *Business Intelligence*, Optima: London.

Ulrich, D. (1989) 'Assessing Human Resource effectiveness: stakeholder, utility and relationship approaches', *Human Resource Planning*, 12(4): 301–15.

Index